American Spring Song

American Spring Song

The Selected Poems of Sherwood Anderson

EDITED BY STUART DOWNS

The Kent State University Press

Kent, Ohio

© 2007 by The Kent State University Press, Kent, Ohio 44242
ALL RIGHTS RESERVED
Library of Congress Catalog Card Number 2006028875
ISBN-10: 0-87338-896-8
ISBN-13: 978-0-87338-896-2
Manufactured in the United States of America

11 10 09 08 07   5 4 3 2 1

LIBRARY OF CONGRESS CATALOGING-IN-PUBLICATION DATA

Anderson, Sherwood, 1876–1941.
  [Poems. Selections]
  American spring song : the selected poems of Sherwood Anderson ;
  edited by Stuart Downs.
      p.   cm.
  Includes bibliographical references.
  ISBN-13: 978-0-87338-896-2 (pbk. : alk. paper) ∞
  ISBN-10: 0-87338-896-8 (pbk. : alk. paper) ∞
  1. Anderson, Sherwood, 1876–1941—Criticism and interpretation.
  I. Downs, Stuart, 1950– II. Title.
  ps3501.n4a6 2007
  813'.52—dc22   2006028875

British Library Cataloging-in-Publication data are available.

Dedicated to the memory of my mother, Virginia Downs.

My heart also goes out to my wife, Kiki; my son, Elliott; and my soul brother, Joe Wenderoth.

CONTENTS

PREFACE AND ACKNOWLEDGMENTS

Of the twenty-three full-length volumes published in Sherwood Anderson's lifetime, two were devoted exclusively to poetry: *Mid-American Chants* in 1918 and *A New Testament* in 1927. Three others contained a mix of prose and poetry: *The Triumph of the Egg* in 1921, *Horses and Men* in 1923, and *Perhaps Women* in 1931. Other volumes devoted to prose often prominently featured poetry at the beginning or in the body of the work. One of the last works to be published while he was living was a small chapbook, *Five Poems,* in 1939.

Critics reviewed Anderson's poetry at the time it was published and for the most part dismissed it completely. Since his death, there has been even less attention paid to his poetic work, with only a few scholarly articles and one full-length study in the form of a master's thesis.[1] The poems have rarely been in print.

The purpose of this volume of selected poems is to reintroduce Sherwood Anderson as an original voice in American poetry and, at the same time, to present his poems to a contemporary audience. As a by-product of this process, perspectives on Anderson, his other writing, the cultural condition of his time, and our own cultural condition are raised to high relief.

* * *

To the friends, teachers, mentors, typists, copy editors, librarians, poets, scholars, editors, literary agents, and institutions who assisted me with this volume, I thank you one and all: David D. Anderson, Carrier Library's Interlibrary Loan staff, Michael Collier, Joanna Craig, Kiki Downs, Mark Facknitz, Susan Facknitz, Harold Ober Associates, Inc., Ben Kamper, the Kent State University Press and their staff, Heather McHugh, Charles E. Modlin, Ron Nelson, the Newberry Library and their staff, Greg Orr, Donna Packard, Monica Petraglia, George Quasha, Jerome Rothenberg, Willis Regier, the Sherwood Anderson Literary Estate Trust, John Skoyles, Elaine Stroupe, Hilary Swinson, Craig Tenney, George Thompson, the Warren Wilson College MFA Program in Creative Writing, Will Underwood, Ellen Bryant Voight, Cole Welter, and Joe Wenderoth.

Ultimately, of course, thank you Sherwood Anderson—for sharing your lyric self.

1. Winfield Scott Lenox, "The Significance of Sherwood Anderson's Poetry" (master's thesis, Loyola Univ., 1961). This study has much in common with this volume of selected poems and is recommended for a more in-depth discussion of the relationship between Anderson's poetic instinct and his prose.

The story of Sherwood Anderson, his life and his writing, has moved in and out of American consciousness both during his lifetime (1876–1941) and since his death. At times it has been well told and remembered; at other times it has been forgotten.

A self-taught man capable of being both businessman and mystic, Anderson's life spanned the fault line of America's transformation from an agrarian to an industrial society. His prose masterwork, *Winesburg, Ohio*, signaled a shift in American writing from external literary structures to internal psychological concerns. In doing so, it captured the undercurrent of estrangement in that time of change. Anderson's life was embroiled in the two faces of the American dream, industrialism and socialism; his story bears repeating in our current time of cultural change.

Born in Camden, Ohio, on September 13, 1876, Anderson and his five siblings saw their father's fate shift as his craft of harness making became obsolete in the face of mass manufacturing. From a dependable provider for his family, Anderson's father became an unreliable housepainter fond of drinking and telling tall tales while Anderson's mother stoically looked on.

As a teenager, Anderson was interested in the popular books of the day but not as interested in school, barely completing the first year of high school. Spurred by the family's need for income, he quit school and became known for his industrious work ethic.

Seeing his fortune aligned to this industrial part of the American dream, Anderson relocated to Chicago from the small town of Clyde, Ohio, in 1896 as he was just turning twenty; instead of upward mobility he found only manual labor. The Spanish-American War brought relief to his situation by giving Anderson the opportunity to serve in the U.S. Army and be stationed briefly in Cuba after the close of the war.

A veteran at age twenty-three, Anderson again tried formal schooling and finished the equivalent of his senior year of high school at Wittenberg Academy in Springfield, Ohio. He did well enough to attend college but instead chose a paying job in Chicago as an advertising solicitor. Anderson's outgoing personality led to success in this position and, in turn, the opportunity to become a copywriter, which allowed him to recognize his talent for writing.

His marriage to Cornelia Lane in 1904 was followed by the birth of three children, Robert, John, and Marion. In terms of livelihood, Anderson left salaried employment to build up and head two businesses, United Factories and Anderson Manufacturing. By 1912, at age thirty-six, he was living the American industrial dream.

However, the part of Anderson that was uncomfortable with the dream he was living began to make itself known. As early as his honeymoon Anderson was writing poetry,[1] and throughout his business career he found time to work on novels. The conflict between his work and his writing became so great that it resulted in a psychological crisis. Although the exact accounts vary, in late November 1912, he abruptly walked out of his business office in Elyria, Ohio, and wandered the state in a dazed condition for four days. Located and identified in Cleveland, he was briefly hospitalized. Regaining his senses, Anderson closed his business and went to Chicago to seek employment; by 1916 he had divorced his wife. Once again working as a copywriter, he set out to become a literary writer.

The timing could not have been more fortuitous. As an antidote to the industrial influences of his youth, Anderson found its antithesis in the egalitarian philosophy of socialism sweeping through Chicago.

Even more fortuitous, Chicago was a hotbed of the modernist movement in the arts and letters. Developing abroad since the late 1800s, early modernism encompassed many experimental styles that, in reaction to the European realist tradition, shared "a high aesthetic self-consciousness and non-representationalism, in which art turns from realism and humanistic representation towards style, technique, and spatial form in pursuit of a deeper penetration of life."[2]

Although many of the writers making a name for themselves in Chicago—Floyd Dell, Theodore Dreiser, Carl Sandburg, Edgar Lee Masters, Vachel Lindsay, and also Anderson—came from humble circumstances in small Midwestern towns and were often self-taught, the city itself was no backwater. Chicago was a major player in the still-developing modernist movement in America during the early 1900s. *The Little Review* and *Poetry,* two of Chicago's new literary magazines at the

1. Hilbert H. Campbell, ed., "Sherwood Anderson: Honeymoon Journal and Other Early Writings, 1904," *The Sherwood Anderson Review* 23 (1998): 49.
2. Malcolm Bradbury and James McFarlane, eds., *Modernism: A Guide to European Literature, 1890–1930* (New York: Penguin, 1991), 25.

time, were publishing James Joyce and Ezra Pound while many of the Chicago writers listed above gained national and international notoriety.

As such, Anderson the writer walked onto a world stage. In a workmanlike way, he wrote and published two novels and one book of poetry. But it was the 1919 publication of his prose work *Winesburg, Ohio,* written in a self-described mystical state at the age of forty-three, that changed American literature. Breaking with conventional realism and literary form, the book was critically acclaimed for its unique short-story structure, which allowed internal psychological concerns to drive the work's gestalt.

In 1921 Anderson received *The Dial*'s first Dial Award for significant achievement by a young American writer. (In subsequent years the award went to T. S. Eliot, William Carlos Williams, and Ezra Pound.) No sooner than he was hailed, the modernist movement closed ranks under the dominance of Eliot and Pound. Both writers privileged reason and intellect over the emotional and native intelligence favored by Anderson. Critics followed suit, and Anderson's ensuing work was often maligned for sentimentalism and lack of form.

Sticking to his own brand of individualism, Anderson continued writing and publishing, eventually becoming disenchanted with the business of making a living as a writer. In 1927 he moved to Virginia and struck out to become a self-sufficient newspaperman by purchasing the Marion Publishing Company in Marion, Virginia. The newspaper business proved financially successful, and even creative, as Anderson, in addition to regular news reporting conceived of, wrote, and filed fanciful reports under the name Buck Fever. At fifty-six Anderson again became restless with his work and turned over the paper to his son in 1932.

Following his divorce from Cornelia Lane in 1904, Anderson married and divorced Tennessee Mitchell and Elizabeth Prall before finding a satisfying soul mate in Eleanor Copenhaver, whom he married in 1933. Together they traveled while he continued to write and publish. In 1941, at the age of sixty-five, the writer died from peritonitis. By the time of his death, Anderson had published twenty-three full-length books, not to mention countless articles, limited-edition volumes, and newspaper stories; he had also written an abundance of unpublished letters to friends.

Today Anderson the writer is known almost exclusively for his prose work: short stories, novels, essays, memoirs, and newspaper articles. What is often left out of his familiar story is that he wrote, published, and was deeply committed to poetry.

* * *

The poems in this collection were published either in literary magazines or in books between 1915 and 1939. In terms of literary context, Anderson's poems reflect a number of his influences: Walt Whitman's poetry, the fitful birth of modernism, and sentimentalism at the turn of the century. His poems should also be viewed from the perspective of Anderson's own personal context: life circumstances, psychological makeup, sense of self, and philosophy of life.

Like most progressive writers of his time, Anderson read Whitman's poetry, directly acknowledging its importance and influence in a letter to Viva Elizabeth Haught in 1935: "I think that any American writer who was not influenced by Walt Whitman would be dead to the work of our most significant poet."[3]

When exactly Anderson read Whitman is open to some speculation, but it was no later than his break with business and subsequent turn to writing. Regardless of the timing, Whitman's sensuality, embrace of nature, vernacular sensibility, and utopian ideals are echoed in the themes and subject matter of Anderson's first volume of poetry and are amplified in his second volume. Anderson found Whitman's mystic vision appealing and, as expressed thematically in a poem in Anderson's *A New Testament*, akin to his own personal philosophy that all creation is one: "You are a man and I would take hold of your hand. You are woman, I would embrace you. You are a child, I would be unashamed to stand in your presence. The flower that is myself has a long stem."[4]

Whitman's influence, as well as the Bible's, is evident in the construction of Anderson's poems. The stanzas are based on the cadences of everyday human speech. Comparing the 1933 edition of Whitman's *Leaves of Grass* (for which Anderson wrote the preface) to Anderson's two full-length volumes of poetry reveals more formal similarities: run-on lines, typographical devices that create separate sections within poems, and italicized stanzas that function as refrains.

---

3. Viva Elizabeth Haught, "The Influence of Walt Whitman on Sherwood Anderson and Carl Sandburg" (master's thesis, Duke Univ., 1936), 41.

4. Sherwood Anderson, *A New Testament* (New York: Boni & Liveright, 1927), 24.

The diction of Anderson's poems also shows a kinship to Whitman. Both Anderson and Whitman revered the everyday person and chose to use vernacular language as the basis of their writing. Choosing the common over high diction had strong ideological overtones for Anderson, who states, "The English had got their books into our schools, their ideas of correct forms of expression were firmly fixed in our minds. Words as commonly used in our writing were in reality an army that marched in a certain array and the generals in command of the army were still English."[5]

Like Whitman, Anderson often referred to his poems as "songs" or "chants." These terms have been used by poets throughout history to imply the emotional, spiritual, and communal properties of a poem. Anderson also chose to call his work "testaments," using that word in poems, as titles for individual poems, and for the title of his second full-length book of poetry *A New Testament.*

In addition to the inheritance of Whitman's influence, Anderson was in the forefront of the first wave of modernism in America. This avant-garde contained the spores of what later would be termed abstractionism, surrealism, and imagism. The heady time also opened up new expressive possibilities for Anderson. A major creative breakthrough came by way of the avatar of modernism, Gertrude Stein (later she and Anderson became lifelong friends).

By the early 1900s Anderson had read Stein's writing, which revealed to him a radical place where form could be abstracted from content. He embraced this writing style. Referring to Stein's *Tender Buttons* (New York: Claire Marie, 1914) Anderson states:

My mind did a kind of jerking flop and after Miss Stein's book had come into my hands I spent days going about with a tablet of paper in my pocket and making new and strange combinations of words. The result was I thought a new familiarity with the words of my own vocabulary.[6]

Here was something purely experimental and dealing with words separated from sense—in the ordinary meaning of the word sense—

5. Sherwood Anderson, *A Story Teller's Story,* ed. Ray Lewis White (Cleveland: Press of Case Western Reserve Univ., 1968), 262.
6. Ibid., 263.

an approach I was sure the poets must often be compelled to make. Was it an approach that would help me? I decided to try it.[7]

His ensuing experimental approach to writing was closer to poetry than prose, and it also embraced qualities similar to visual art. Anderson's intimacy in the interdisciplinary sensibility of the era is relevant here. In addition to his writing, Anderson was enthralled with painting, both producing and occasionally exhibiting his own work. He was also friends with America's groundbreaking artists, such as Alfred Steiglitz, Georgia O'Keefe, and Arthur Dove. He shared with them, through Stein's influence, an understanding of the creative expression based on abstraction that broke with the representational mode of the previous generation. For Anderson, "words . . . were as the colors used by the painter. . . . Words were the surfaces."[8]

Abstraction in writing was one thing; however, on an even more elemental level, Stein provided Anderson with the means to apply such a concept to his own sense of self: "All of the more beautiful and clear, the more plangent and radiant writing I have done, has all been done by a kind of second personality that at such times takes possession of me. . . . This, I think, might bring me to what Stein did for me. . . . [S]he taught me to recognize the second person in myself, the poet writing person, so that I could occasionally release that one."[9]

This "second person" can be referred to as Anderson's lyric self. In the past, poetry was stylistically defined as lyric poetry, narrative poetry, or dramatic poetry. Lyric poetry, based on the emotional sensibility of the poet, was gaining popularity at the turn of the century. For Anderson lyric poetry was not a style but a recognition of self. The "poet writing person"—the lyric self—was the most elemental aspect of Anderson's personal response to the world; a response that would break with intellectual, external, egotistic, linear, and cultural instincts prevalent in the literary and industrial climate of the time, as opposed to emotional, internal, selfless, nonlinear, and individualistic instincts that Anderson found more true to himself. Anderson makes such a lyric self known

7. Ibid., 260–61.
8. Ibid., 261.
9. Sherwood Anderson, *Letters of Sherwood Anderson*, ed. Howard Mumford Jones and Walter B. Rideout (Boston: Little, Brown, 1953), 300.

through his poetry when he writes in "Song of Industrial America," "I'm a song myself, the broken end of a song myself."[10]

Anderson's lyric self is evident in parts of his earlier *Mid-American Chants,* as well as in *Winesburg, Ohio* and the works that followed; it is the defining element of his memorable writing, not just his poetry. In his poetry, the voice of the lyric self is predominantly in first person and features no character, narrator, mask, or persona, meaning Anderson apparently speaks for himself. In his prose, the voice of the lyric self is in first, second, or third person, and Anderson speaks through a character, narrator, mask, or persona.

The surreal is another modernist tendency present in varying degrees throughout Anderson's poetry. It can be seen particularly through the expression of the irrational, the juxtaposition of incongruous images and the evocation of altered states of mind. For example, Anderson evokes the surreal in only fourteen words by a quick, unimaginable (but unforgettable) image, as in "One Who Looked Up at the Sky," "It would be strange if, by a thought, a man could make Illinois pregnant."[11] On a grander scale, the surreal manifests through a recurring metaphor that creates the hallucinatory atmosphere in Anderson's poem "Testament of an Old Man."

> My brain is a hound that has come out of its kennel. . . .
> My awakened brain is a hound dog come out of its kennel. It is a hound dog, white and silent and swift. . . .
> My hound brain is a whispering wind. It runs backward and forward. . . .
> My hound mind has seen cities rise out of the plains and it has seen cities destroyed. . . .
> Look how it runs. . . . Someday it will not return to its kennel.[12]

Anderson's surrealistic instinct is challenging to place, and most of his poems do not fit in context with the formal surrealist movement as pronounced by André Breton in 1924. Prior to Breton's pronouncement, Anderson had learned to play with words in a somewhat surrealist way from the example of Gertrude Stein's writing. He also spent time in Paris

---

10. Sherwood Anderson, *Mid-American Chants* (New York: John Lane, 1918), 18.
11. Anderson, *Testament,* 11.
12. Ibid., 32–37.

in 1921, which was a hotbed of surrealism, and his poetry of the early 1920s in *The Little Review* is especially flush with surreal flourishes. Anderson owned copies of Charles Baudelaire's poetry, which is often cited as an influence on the surrealist movement. However, there is no evidence that Anderson knew the main proponents of surrealism or had an affinity with their stated philosophies. Whether or not his style stemmed from European literary origin or his own psychological mindset, it is obvious Anderson had no qualms about altering reality.

Anderson's creative altering of reality was at odds with his penchant for concrete detail, especially in its imagism. This distinctive characteristic is present in his published poetry and prose and is put to diverse use as exemplified in the following two examples. In his first volume of poetry, a poem of only twenty-nine words develops from a single image, "Against the cold white night a stain of red . . . / My unborn son is dead."[13] This concrete image in "Unborn" is constructed simply by the color red on white; its content heightened because the red color is a stain; and that it relates to the complexity of an unborn son, which is left for the reader to resolve.

In contrast, the lengthy poem "The Man in the Brown Coat" possesses an abstract texture but depends on a series of highly concrete images to achieve that effect:

There is a yellow house opposite our house. My wife goes out a side door and passes along our street between our house and the yellow house.

The window before my desk makes a little framed place like a picture. The yellow house across the street makes a solid background of yellow.

The side door of my house bangs. There is a moment of waiting. My wife's face floats across the yellow background of the picture.[14]

Although the overall texture of this poem is one of abstract estrangement, Anderson achieves this effect with a series of highly concrete images that are as descriptive as they are impersonal in these examples: "a yellow

13. Anderson, *Chants,* 53.
14. Anderson, *Testament,* 73.

house opposite our house," "the window before my desk," and "the side door of my house bangs."

On one level, this knack for image making was intuitive; yet on another level, Anderson was aware of his talent and worked to develop it. Beyond the image in the poem is the image created by the poem. His work draws on the Chinese technique of the short stop, which Anderson himself knew about: "The old Chinese used to write a thing called 'the short stop.' The notion was to touch something off and then let it complete itself in the reader."[15] Anderson employed this technique by recasting lengthy poems originally published in *The Little Review* into dramatically shorter poems, some of which were then collected in *A New Testament*.

In addition to the literary context of Anderson's poetry, it is important to recognize the personal context. Anderson was strongly individualistic and resisted being defined by elitist sensibility. Self-taught, he read both classic and popular works while growing up and absorbed and practiced the folk art of storytelling.

It is hard to pin down the origin of his sentimentalism during this early naïveté. Sentimentalism would be a charge critics would later make of his mature work. From teenager to young adult, his reading was a mix of materials, some of which reinforced his melodramatic impulses. He writes about his reading habits, "I read greedily everything that came into my hands. Laura Jean Libbey, Walter Scott, Harriet Beecher Stowe, Henry Fielding, Shakespeare, Jules Verne, Balzac, the Bible, Stephen Crane, dime novels, Cooper, Stevenson, our own Mark Twain and Howells and later Whitman."[16] As he developed and read more purely literary works, he still found sentimentalism reinforced in the genteel belle art tradition of the time. And despite the progressive influence of Walt Whitman, Anderson would also absorb Whitman's occasional emotional gushes. For example, Whitman repeats the line "Pioneers! O Pioneers!" twenty-six times in a poem of the same name in the 1933 edition of *Leaves of Grass*, of which Anderson wrote the introduction.[17]

Anderson's sentimentalism would be easier to dismiss from a literary standpoint if he had grown out of it or had learned to revise to allow for

15. Sherwood Anderson, *The Writer's Book*, ed. Martha Mulroy Curry (Metuchen, N.J.: Scarecrow Press, 1975), 278.

16. Anderson, *Story Teller's Story*, 117.

17. Walt Whitman, *Leaves of Grass*, ed. Charles Cullen (New York: Thomas Y. Crowell, 1933), 143–47.

a more sophisticated writing style. But this was not Anderson: it was not external evocations of sentiment he was seeking to express but internal, emotional truth. If in this desire he overreached, as witnessed in his use of clichéd language and melodramatic ploys popular at the time in *Mid-American Chants,* then so be it. He took a risk with his writing style and defends his *Mid-American Chants* in one of his letters: "It is of course all amateurish . . . but I am and I hope will remain that."[18] This non-aesthetic stance was subject to misinterpretation as pure sentimentalism when, to him, it was worth risking in staking out the authentic emotional state he believed to be fundamental to human experience and the source of his poetry.

In other words, Anderson's personal context in terms of his sense of self and philosophy of life took precedence over purely literary concerns. He believed strongly, if not mystically, in the creative response of his own existence. This existence was one where life was a process. It was not separated from art or literature; emotion and empathy were privileged over more traditional, craft-oriented approaches to writing, whether it be poetry or prose: "I refused to quibble over words and sentences put down. That did not interest me"[19]; "It is possible at times, I think, to get into the flow, the under voices becoming audible"[20]; "I have a belief that in this matter of form it is largely a matter of depth of feeling. How deeply do you feel it. Feel it deeply enough and you will be torn inside and driven on until form comes."[21] Emotion being one part of process, empathy was the other:

> The man is there in the field with his horses, and sometimes everything is fused. The field is in the man and his horses. The man is in his horses. The horses are in the man. There is something lovely, a fact. But I am closest to the man. I know no way to tell the horses or the fields. It seems to me that I do want the man to feel as I at the moment feel. There is at least hope that I may tell him in a poem or painting.[22]

Being in the moment was what was important to Anderson, as he shared with a writer asking for advice, "it was then you were writing

18. Anderson, *Letters,* 20.
19. Ibid., 446.
20. Ibid., 445.
21. Ibid., 387.
22. Ibid., 362.

well. It may have been because you had forgotten you were writing and were thinking only of the moment."[23] From Anderson's standpoint, self-conscious refinement of writing was often a deterrent to being authentic: better to be amateurish, to acknowledge "crudity,"[24] or, rather than strive to make a perfect poem, better to simply render "just the broken ends."[25]

The result was writing (poetry, prose, or experimental) that did not lend itself to the critic's traditional dualistic analysis of form and content. Anderson states the case that would make most critics cringe: "I think it would be a great mistake to waste anytime at all thinking of 'form' as form. . . . Form is, of course, content. It is nothing else, can be nothing else. A tree has bark, fiber, sap, leaves, limbs, twigs. It can grow and exist and not grow in the soil of your own being. . . . The great thing is to let yourself be the tree, the sky, the earth. . . . My meaning is that life is not so separated from art."[26] Such statements, more philosophical than critical, simply weren't in keeping with the literary thinking of the time.

What his writing did lend itself to was a response that was boldly all Anderson. If the polarities of the literary context he absorbed can be reduced to the push of the concrete (Whitman) and the pull of the abstract (Stein), Anderson's response to such magnetic yet antithetical sensibilities was to embrace both. Like Whitman, he was empathetic; like Stein, he was estranged. Unlike Whitman, his quest for transcendence brought the pain of non-transcendence; unlike Stein, his response to that pain was not intellectually cool but emotionally warm.

The fusion of the concrete and the abstract made Anderson's life unique and his writing open to simultaneity: dark and light; pathos and hope; pain and love; and, anticipating Martin Buber's philosophy of life, I and Thou. Anderson's was an existential response not of despair but of a fierce affirmation of life and death.

More than the literary devices of tone, voice, or style, it is the lyric self, "the poet writing person," that defines all of his writing.[27] It is particularly resonant in his poetry; he does not speak through a character or a narrator but directly from that lyric self to the reader, as in, "I am born—why am I not born?"[28] In essence, the simple statement and question strike to the

---

23. Ibid., 449.
24. Sherwood Anderson, "An Apology for Crudity," *Dial* 63 (Nov. 8, 1917): 437–38.
25. Anderson, *Writer's Book*, 278.
26. Anderson, *Letters*, 202.
27. Ibid., 300.
28. Anderson, *Testament*, 118.

heart of existentialism. Rather than answering the question, it leaves the reader to struggle with the question of existence.

The nakedness of this lyric self certainly made critics who were used to urbane, impersonal modernism uneasy with his poetry. In fact, it made Anderson himself uneasy, as he noted in a letter to Mary Chryst Anderson late in life, "the thing least to be desired in this world is to be known as poet."[29] In the same sentence, Anderson openly acknowledged a penetrating revelation: "The truth is that I have always known I was essentially the poet."[30]

Many critics acknowledge this lyric self that is at the heart of Anderson's most enduring prose. It is this lyric self in its boldness, passion, tenderness, outrageousness, and vulnerability that allows Anderson's best poetry to be discovered by another generation, at a time when individuals are confronted by cultural hegemony, societal transformation, and personal estrangement. For a contemporary audience seeking self-definition and who has been left numb by self-doubt, the lasting testament of *American Spring Song* is its affirmation of the lyric self; both Sherwood Anderson's and our own.

29. Anderson, *Letters*, 300.

30. Ibid. Appearing in the same letter, this quotation and the preceding one are quite provocative and deserve more attention than the scope of this introduction can provide. Anderson's poetic ambiversion is present throughout his literary career. On the one hand, he would deride poetry: "The many men have told me they wanted leisure to write poetry. Great God! The amount of physical labor needed to make a man widely known as a poet of merit is infinitesimal. All the actual physical labor of writing done by the greatest and most profound of poets could be done by an average newspaperman during any average month of work." Sherwood Anderson, *Sherwood Anderson's Notebook* (New York: Boni & Liveright, 1926), 61. On the other hand, he would also elevate poetry: "The story of Wing Biddlebaum's hands is worth a book in itself. Sympathetically set forth it would tap many strange, beautiful qualities in obscure men. It is a job for a poet." Sherwood Anderson, *Winesburg, Ohio* (New York: B. W. Huebsch, 1919), 29.

There are numerous plausible and documentable reasons for Anderson's vacillation, ranging from shyness to the need for income derived from more commercially popular prose to a psychological defense mechanism to his penchant for mythologizing himself. Further investigation and assessment of Anderson's poetic nature and its impact on all his writing is long overdue. See Lenox, "The Significance of Sherwood Anderson's Poetry."

NOTES ON SELECTION OF POEMS AND EDITING

Poems in this volume were selected from Sherwood Anderson's published work and represent approximately one-third of his total published poems.

I used aesthetic criteria as a guide in selecting the most resonant poems. In this regard, the focus was on poems that possessed clarity of voice, freshness of diction, coherence of form (traditional or experimental), impact of image, and originality of thought and feeling.

For the most part, the criteria did not emphasize poems that could not stand apart from their historical context; poems that displayed clichéd language popular at the time; or poems whose flaws, such as overt symbolism or awkward experimentalism, distracted from the poem as a whole. At the same time, aesthetically strong poems with some of these flawed tendencies were included to provide readers with a more complete understanding of Anderson's historical, literary, and personal contexts. This delicate balance in selection, along with its primarily chronological presentation, serves as a microcosm of Anderson's development and achievement as a poet.

Anderson published poems in books and magazines. Some of these works were experimental and were not consistently labeled as poems by Anderson or in the magazine's table of contents. Only later when they were collected and published in book form were they definitively referred to as poems. Any work exhibiting this irregular categorization that Anderson allowed to be published was considered for inclusion in this volume and, in some cases, has been included.

By the time the work that had appeared in magazines was gathered into a volume, there were often revisions Anderson made. (In at least one instance, "The Man in the Brown Coat" was published three times in a three different versions appearing in *Little Review* VI, *The Triumph of the Egg,* and *A New Testament.*) As long as it was published, each version was considered valid for inclusion without the presumption that the last version was the best.[1]

Of these previously published versions, many originally appeared in *The Little Review.* Most of this material was long experimental work often composed of numerous separate sections, some of which were linked

---

1. Highly recommended for a listing of these variants is Raymond D. Gozzi's "A Bibliography of Sherwood Anderson's Contributions to Periodicals, 1914–1946," "The Newberry Library Bulletin," 2nd ser., no. 2 (Dec. 1948).

contextually together and some of which were not. Anderson returned to these experimental works, dramatically revising some of them by deleting parts of a section, leaving a shorter version that displayed more emotion and/or ambiguity. These revised versions were then included in *A New Testament,* many of which have been included in this volume. I also considered including in this volume his work published in *The Little Review* that he did not revise, if it could exist independently of its initial context (much like the sections selected by Anderson in *A New Testament*). Some of this work is included.

Other than what was considered to be poems, I reviewed most of Anderson's other published work (short stories, novels, letters, memoirs, introductions, diaries, and journals) to see if, for the sake of their general experimental bent, some of them should be included. There are many short flashes and sustained passages of poetic effect in the prose works noted above. However, in my opinion, few cohere to form a work that is first and foremost of poetic quality and that is written in first person (like most of his poems). Two exceptions, "Little Sister" (originally published as a short story) and "Forward" (originally published as the forward to *Horses and Men*), do cohere and are in first person and have been included in this volume. In addition to their poetic quality based on the aforementioned aesthetic criteria, they underscore Anderson's instinct to transcend the traditional boundaries of poetry and prose.

Typesetting Anderson's work was a challenge due to the varied lineation of his published poems. These poems were consistent in that they were composed of elements that would appear in print as poetic lines (consisting of a single sentence or phrase), poetic passages (consisting of more than one sentence), or a mix of lines and passages. The nuances of what were lines, what were passages, and the spaces that functioned as line breaks and stanza breaks were extremely important, as they served as an internal, mental syntax. The external representation of the poetic lines and passages on the page produced a number of possible lineations, all of which accurately reflected the poem.

Anderson experimented with different approaches to lineation, three of which appear most frequently in his published poems:

1) All lines and passages begin flush left. If they run beyond the right margin, they are indented on the following line:

_____

_____

2) All lines and passages begin indented. If they run beyond the right margin, they are not indented on the following line but are positioned flush left:

---

3) All lines and passages begin flush left. If they run beyond the right margin, they are not indented on the following line but are positioned flush left:

Anderson's experimental nature was such that on occasion the lineation of a single poem might be changed in two different published forms. Being consistent with his experimental inconsistency it was possible for a single volume, such as Anderson's *The Triumph of the Egg* (New York: B. W. Huebsch, 1921), to exhibit three different approaches to lineation.

The most dramatic example of his varied lineation, however, is Anderson's use of two different approaches in his first and second books of poetry. Akin to Walt Whitman's *Leaves of Grass,* Anderson's first book of poems, *Mid-American Chants,* was typeset like lineation 1, as seen above.

Anderson's second book of poems, *A New Testament,* was typeset according to the example of lineation 2. While composing this book, Anderson was writing the introduction to Gertrude Stein's *Geography and Plays,* which used the same type of lineation as *A New Testament.* Add a most unusual and intrusive type font to the second volume and you certainly have an unfamiliar looking and rather unreadable book, at least from a visual standpoint.[2]

2. The question arises as to where these variations in lineation and choice of type font originated: with Anderson or with the publisher. The typesetting and type font in the second volume are so different from Anderson's first volume that it might have been done at the whim of the publisher. It is possible that the type font might have been the publisher's idea, but it appears that Anderson himself was devoted to the change in lineation. A typescript of *A New Testament* in the Newberry Library supports Anderson's part in the change in lineation. At the same time, early handwritten and manuscript copies of *A New Testament* at the Newberry show that Anderson occasionally employed other approaches to lineation. Regardless of his experimental tendency, it decidedly rigidified into a conscious choice in the final published version of *A New Testament.* If it did not distract the audience from a coherent reading of Anderson's poems, we could easily dismiss the choice of type font and lineation. More research needs to be done before these choices can be better understood. For now, it is simplest to say that in terms of lineation the first volume resembles Walt Whitman's *Leaves of Grass* (ed. Charles Cullen, New York: Thomas Y. Crowell, 1933), while the second volume resembles Gertrude Stein's *Geography and Plays* (Boston: Four Seas, 1922).

For this volume of selected poems, I made the editorial decision to standardize the presentation of Anderson's poems to fit with the form of his first volume of poems (lineation 1). This standardization was done not only to ensure readability but also to preserve the nuances of his lines and stanzas while remaining clear to readers. These changes were made with the knowledge that Anderson himself consciously approved of the format changes between his first and second volumes of poetry.

I also made the editorial decision to standardize stanza breaks in poems constructed almost entirely of poetic passages, in order to make them consistent with the majority of similar poems in *Mid-American Chants* and *A New Testament*. This standardization was not applied to poems constructed of a mixture of poetic passages and poetic lines, where the enjambment created by the lack of stanza breaks was important to creating a desired rhythm. The intent of this standardization was, as before, to make this volume more easily readable.

The first poem in this volume, "American Spring Song," and the last poem, "Assurance," are both from Anderson's first book of poems *Mid-American Chants*. They are separated from the rest of the poems in this volume to serve as a prologue and epilogue. The rest of the poems appear chronologically according to their original date of publication.

AMERICAN SPRING SONG

In the spring, when winds blew and farmers were plowing fields,
It came into my mind to be glad because of my brutality.

Along a street I went and over a bridge.

I went through many streets in my city and over many bridges.

Men and women I struck with my fists and my hands began to bleed.

Under a bridge I crawled and stood trembling with joy
At the river's edge.

Because it was spring and soft sunlight came through the cracks of the
    bridge
I tried to understand myself.

Out of the mud at the river's edge I moulded myself a god,
A grotesque little god with a twisted face,
A god for myself and my men.

You see now, brother, how it was.

I was a man with clothes made by a Jewish tailor,
Cunningly wrought clothes, made for a nameless one.

I wore a white collar and some one had given me a jeweled pin
To wear at my throat.
That amused and hurt me too.

No one knew that I knelt in the mud beneath the bridge
In the city of Chicago.

You see I am whispering my secret to you.

I want you to believe in my insanity and to understand that I love God—

That's what I want.
And then, you see, it was spring
And soft sunlight came through the cracks of the bridge.

I had been long alone in a strange place where no gods came.

Creep, men, and kiss the twisted face of my mud god.

I'll not hit you with my bleeding fists.

I'm a twisted god myself.

It is spring and love has come to me—
Love has come to me and to my men.

Mid-American Chants, 1918

SISTER

The young artist is a woman, and at evening she comes to talk to me in my room. She is my sister, but long ago she has forgotten that and I have forgotten.

Neither my sister nor I live in our father's house, and among all my brothers and sisters I am conscious only of her. The others have positions in the city and in the evening go home to the house where my sister and I once lived. My father is old and his hands tremble. He is not concerned about me, but my sister who lives alone in a room in a house on North Dearborn Street has caused him much unhappiness.

Into my room in the evening comes my sister and sits upon a low couch by the door. She sits cross-legged and smokes cigarettes. When she comes it is always the same—she is embarrassed and I am embarrassed. When she was quite young she was awkward and boyish and tore her clothes climbing trees. It was after that her strangeness began to be noticed. Day after day she would slip away from the house and go to walk in the streets. She became a devout student and made such rapid strides in her classes that my mother—who to tell the truth is fat and uninteresting—spent the days worrying. My sister, she declared, would end by having brain fever.

When my sister was fifteen years old she announced to the family that she was about to take a lover. I was away from home at the time, on one of the wandering trips that have always been a passion to me.

My sister came into the house, where the family were seated at the table, and, standing by the door, said she had decided to spend the night with a boy of sixteen who was the son of a neighbor.

The neighbor boy knew nothing of my sister's intentions. He was at home from college, a tall, quiet, blue-eyed fellow, with his mind set upon foot-ball. To my family my sister explained that she would go to the boy and tell him of her desires. Her eyes flashed and she stamped her foot upon the floor.

My father whipped my sister. Taking her by the arm he led her into the stable at the back of the house. He whipped her with a long black whip that always stood upright in the whipsocket of the carriage in which, on Sundays, my mother and father drove about the streets of our suburb. After the whipping my father was ill.

I am wondering how I know so intimately all the details of the whipping of my sister. Neither my father nor my sister have told me of it. Perhaps sometime, as I sat dreaming in a chair, my mother gossiped of the whipping. It would be like her to do that, and it is a trick of my mind never to remember her figure in connection with the things she has told me.

After the whipping in the stable my sister was quite changed. The family sat tense and quiet at the table and when she came into the house she laughed and went upstairs to her own room. She was very quiet and well-behaved for several years and when she was twenty-one inherited some money and went to live alone in the house on North Dearborn Street. I have a feeling that the walls of our house told me the story of the whipping. I could never live in the house afterwards and came away at once to this room where I am now and where my sister comes to visit me.

And so there is my sister in my room and we are embarrassed. I do not look at her but turn my back and begin writing furiously. Presently she is on the arm of my chair with her arm about my neck.

I am the world and my sister is the young artist in the world. I am afraid the world will destroy her. So furious is my love of her that the touch of her hand makes me tremble.

My sister would not write as I am now writing. How strange it would be to see her engaged in anything of the kind. She would never give the slightest bit of advice to anyone. If you were dying and her advice would save you she would say nothing.

My sister is the most wonderful artist in the world, but when she is with me I do not remember that. When she has talked of her adventures, up from the chair I spring and go ranting about the room. I am half blind with anger, thinking perhaps that strange, furtive looking youth, with whom I saw her walking yesterday in the streets, has had her in his arms. The flesh of my sister is sacred to me. If anything were to happen to her body I think I should kill myself in sheer madness.

In the evening after my sister is gone I do not try to work anymore. I pull my couch to the opening by the window and lie down. It is then a little that I begin to understand my sister. She is the artist right to adventure in the world, to be destroyed in the adventure, if that be necessary, and I, on my couch, am the worker in the world, blinking up at the stars that can be seen from my window when my couch is properly arranged.

The Little Review, 1915

UNTITLED

I am mature, a man child, in America, in the west, in the great valley of the Mississippi. My head arises above the corn fields. I stand up among the new corn.

I am a child, a confused child in a confused world. There are no clothes made that fit me. The minds of men cannot clothe me. Great projects arise within me. I have a brain and it is cunning and shrewd.

I want leisure to become beautiful but there is no leisure. Men should bathe me with prayers and with weeping but there are no men.

Now—from now—from today I shall do deeds of fiery meaning. Songs shall arise in my throat and hurt me.

I am a little thing, a tiny little thing on the vast prairies. I know nothing. My mouth is dirty. I cannot tell what I want. My feet are sunk in the black swampy land but I am a lover. I love life. In the end love shall save me.

The days are long. It rains. It snows. I am an old man. I am sweeping the ground where my grave shall be.

Look upon me, my beloved, my lover who does not come. I am raw and bleeding, a new thing in a new world. I run swiftly over bare fields. Listen! There is the sound of the tramping of many feet. Life is dying in me. I am old and palsied. I am just at the beginning of my life.

Do you not see that I am old, oh my beloved? Do you not understand that I cannot sing, that my songs choke me? Do you not see that I am so young I cannot find the word in the confusion of words?

Epigraph to "From Chicago," Seven Arts, 1917

SONG OF THE SOUL OF CHICAGO

On the bridges, on the bridges, swooping and rising, whirling and
circling. Back to the bridges, always the bridges.

I'll talk forever. I'm damned if I'll sing. Don't you see that mine is not
a singing people? We're just a lot of muddy things caught up by the
stream. You can't fool us. Don't we know ourselves?

Here we are, out here in Chicago. You think we're not humble? You're
a liar. We are like the sewage of our town, swept up stream by a
kind of mechanical triumph—that's what we are.

On the bridges, on the bridges. Wagons and motors, horses and
men—not flying—just tearing along and swearing.

By God we'll love each other or die trying. We'll get to understanding
too. In some grim way our own song shall work through.

We'll stay down in the muddy depths of our stream. We will. There
can't any poet come out here and sit on the shaky rail of our ugly
bridges and sing us into paradise.

We're finding out. That's what I want to say. We'll get at our
own thing out here or die for it. We're going down, numberless
thousands of us, into ugly oblivion. We know that.

But say, bards, you keep off our bridges. Keep out of our dreams,
dreamers. We want to give this democracy thing they talk so big
about a whirl. We want to see if we are any good out here—we
Americans from all over hell. That's what we want.

Others, 1917

SONG OF INDUSTRIAL AMERICA

They tell themselves so many little lies, my Beloved. Now wait, little hand. You can't sing. We are standing in a crowd, by a bridge, in the West. Hear the voices. Turn around. Let's go home. I am tired. They tell themselves so many little lies.

You remember, in the night we arose. We were young. There was smoke in the passage and you laughed. Was it good—that black smoke? Look away—to the streams and the lake. We're alive. See my hand, how it trembles on the rail.

Here is song, here in America, here now, in our time. Now wait. I'll go to the train. I'll not swing off into tunes. I'm all right. I just want to talk.

You watch my hand on the rail of this bridge. I press down. The blood goes down, there. That steadies me; it makes me all right. Now here is how it's going to come—the song, I mean. I've watched things, men and faces, I know.

First, there are the broken things, myself and the others. I don't mind that. I'm gone, shot to pieces. I'm a part of the scheme. I'm the broken end of a song myself. We are all that, here in the West, here in Chicago. Tongues clatter against teeth. There is nothing but shrill screams and a rattle. That had to be. It's a part of the scheme.

Souls, dry souls, rattle around.
Winter of song. Winter of song.

Now, faint little voice, do lift up. They are swept away in the void. That's true enough. It had to be so from the very first.

Pshaw, I'm steady enough—let me alone. Keokuk, Tennessee, Michigan, Chicago, Kalamazoo—don't the names in this country fairly make you drunk? We'll stand by this brown stream for hours. I'll not be swept away—watch my hand, how steady it is. To catch this song and sing it would do much, make much clear.

Come close to me, warm little thing. It is night. I am cold. When I was
a boy in my village, here in the West, I always knew all the old men.
How sweet they were—quite biblical too—makers of wagons and
harness and plows, sailors and soldiers and pioneers. We got Walt
and Abraham out of that lot.

Then a change came.

Drifting along. Drifting along.
Winter of song. Winter of song.

You know my city, Chicago-triumphant—factories and marts and the
roar of machines—horrible, terrible, ugly and brutal.

It crushed things down and down. Nobody wanted to hurt. They didn't
want to hurt me or you. They were caught themselves. I know the
old men here—millionaires. I've always known old men all my life.
I'm old myself. You would never guess how old I am.

Can a singer arise and sing in this smoke and grime? Can he keep his
throat clear? Can his courage survive?

I'll tell you what it is—now you be still. To hell with you. I'm an old
empty barrel floating in the stream—that's what I am. You stand
away. I've come to life. My arms lift up. I begin to swim.

Hell and damnation—turn me loose! The floods come on. That isn't
the roar of the trains at all. It's the flood, the terrible, horrible flood
turned loose.

Winter of song. Winter of song.
Carried along. Carried along.

Now in the midst of the broken waters of my civilization rhythm
begins. Clear above the flood I raise my ringing voice. In the

disorder and darkness of the night, in the wind and the washing waves, I shout to my brothers—lost in the flood.

Little faint beginnings of things—old things dead, sweet old things—a life lived in Chicago, in the West, in the whirl of industrial America.

God knows you might have become something else—just like me. You might have made soft little tunes, written cynical little ditties, eh? Why the devil didn't you make some money and own an automobile?

Do you believe—now listen—I do. Say, you—now listen! Do you believe the hand of God reached down to me in the flood? I do. 'Twas like a streak of fire along my back. That's a lie? Of course. The face of God looked down at me over the rim of the world.

Don't you see we are all a part of something, here in the West? We are trying to break through. I'm a song myself, the broken end of a song myself.

We have to sing, you see, here in the darkness. All men have to sing— poor broken things. We have to sing here in the darkness in the roaring flood. We have to find each other. Have you courage tonight for a song? Lift your voices. Come.

Poetry, 1917

SONG OF THE DRUNKEN BUSINESS MAN

Don't try, little one, to keep hold of me.
Go home! There's a place for you by the fire.
Age is waiting to welcome you, love—
Go home and sit by the fire.

Into the naked street I ran,
Roaring and bellowing like a cow;
Shaking the walls of the houses down,
Proclaiming my dream of black desire.

Eighteen letters in a pigeon-hole.
Eighteen letters in a pigeon-hole.

If there's a thing in this world that's good it's guts.
I'm a blackbird hovering over the lands:
Go home! Let me alone.

Eighteen letters in a pigeon-hole.
Eighteen letters in a pigeon-hole.

Do you know, little dove, I admire your lips—
They're so red.
What are you doing out in the street?
Take my arm! Look at me!
Ah, you be gone. I'm sixty-five years old tonight,
Now what's the use of beginning again.

Eighteen letters in a pigeon-hole.
Eighteen letters in a pigeon-hole.

Well, I'm tired. I ache. What's the use?
I can't meet the note. I have a son.
Let's go home. It's twelve o'clock.
I'm going to get that boy into West Point yet.

Eighteen letters in a pigeon-hole.
Eighteen letters in a pigeon-hole.

Poetry, 1917

EVENING SONG

My song will rest while I rest. I struggle along. I'll get back to the corn
   and the open fields. Don't fret, love, I'll come out all right.

Back of Chicago the open fields. Were you ever there—trains coming
   toward you out of the East—streaks of light on the long gray plains?
   Many a song—aching to sing.

I've got a gray and ragged brother in my breast—that's a fact. Back
   of Chicago the open fields—long trains go west too—in the silence.
   Don't fret, love. I'll come out all right.

Poetry, 1917

NIGHT WHISPERS

Just midnight quiet and a sundered cloud,—mother I live—
Aching and waiting to work my way through.

You of the long and the gaunt—silent and grim you stood.
Terribly sweet the touch of your hand—mother, reach down.

Grey the walls and long the waiting—grey the age dust on the floor.
If they whip and beat us, little mother, need we care?

Mid-American Chants, 1918

REMINISCENT SONG

Now you are dear to me,
Now my beloved.
You are the one that I did not take.
Even then,
When my body was young,
When the sweetness of you made me drunk,
You are the one that I did not take.

All that is old came into me,
That night by the bush and the stairs in the dark.
Yours were the lips I did not kiss,
Yours the love that I kept.

Long and long I have walked alone.
Past the cornfields and over the bridge,
Sucking the sweetness out of nights,
Dreaming things that have made me old
And young,
Since that night.

Faring away down a lonely road
Now you must go, my beloved,
Thinking your thoughts in the bitter nights,
You that I loved and did not take.

Mid-American Chants, 1918

THE LOVER

All night she walked and dreamed on the frozen road,
She the insane one, feeling not thinking.
All night she walked and wanted to kill,
Wanted to love and kill.

What did she want?
Nobody knew.
None of us knew why she wanted
To kill.

We were the heavy ones, heavy and sure.
The wind in the cornfields moved us not.
We the Americans, worthy and sure,
Worthy and sure of ourselves.

Tom killed his brother on Wednesday night,
Back of the corncrib, under the hill.
Then she ran to him, sobbing and calling,
She who had loved and could not kill.

Mid-American Chants, 1918

THE STRANGER

Her eyes are like the seeds of melons. Her breasts are thin and she
  walks awkwardly. I am in love with her.
With her I have adventured into a new love. In all the world there is no
  such love as I have for her.
I took hold of her shoulder and walked beside her. We went out of the
  city into the fields. By the still road we went and it was night. We
  were alone together.
The bones of her shoulder are thin. The sharp bone of her shoulder has
  left a mark on my hand.
I am come up into the wind like a ship. Her thin hand is laid hold of
  me. My land where the corn nods has become my land.
I am come up into the wind like a ship and the thin hand of woman is
  laid hold of me.

Mid-American Chants, 1918

UNBORN

Swift across the night a little cry,
Against the cold white night a stain of red.
The moon dips down,
The dull winds blow.
My unborn son is dead.

Mid-American Chants, 1918

SONG OF THE LOVE OF WOMEN

Have you nothing to offer but bread and your bodies—
Women, my women?
Long nights I have lain by you, sleepless and thinking—
Sisters, my sisters.

In the doorway of the warehouse a tiny twisted body.
Hark, the night is long. Let us talk. One! Two! Three!
One! Two! Three! March! March away!

Come to me, sisters, come home to the cornfields—
Long have I ached for you, body and brain.
Have you nothing to offer but bread and your bodies—
How long must I wait for you, sisters, in vain?

Mid-American Chants, 1918

THE BEAM

Eighteen men stood by me in my fall—long men—strong men—see the oil on their boots.

I was a guest in the house of my people. Through the years I clung, taking hold of their hands in the darkness. It rained and the roar of machines was incessant. Into the house of my people quiet would not come.

Eighteen men stood by me in my fall. Through their breasts bars were driven. With wailing and with weeping I ran back and forth. Then I died. Out of the door of the house of my people I ran. But the eighteen men stood by me in my fall.

Mid-American Chants, 1918

SONG TO THE LAUGH

All night we lay in the cold and the rain in the midst of the laughter,
The laughter of weaklings,
The laughter of women,
The laughter of those who were strong.

At the end of the lane we lay, beyond the roar and the rattle.

Hark! In the silence the laughter!

Strong men creeping,
Old men creeping,
Old men and children, creeping and creeping—
Far away in the darkness.

Edward, my son,
Thomas, my man,
Why do you creep all night in the darkness?
Why do you creep and wait to strike at night in the darkness?

Nine! Ten! Twelve!
Nine! Ten! Twelve!

Take the knife from the shield and strike in the darkness.
Strike, man! Strike!

All night we lay in the cold and wet at the edge of the darkness.

Trembling with fear we prepared to welcome the knife thrust.
Then we kissed and our bodies caressed.
We prepared, my beloved, to add our voices to those of the others.
In the cold and wet we crept and laughed in the darkness.

Mid-American Chants, 1918

WE ENTER IN

Now you see, brothers, here in the West, here's how it is—
We stand and fall, we hesitate—
It is all new to us,
To kill, to take a fellow's life.
Uh!—a nauseous fever takes the light away.

Now we stand up and enter in.
The baseness of the deed we too embrace.
We go in dumbly—into that dark place.
The germ of death we take into our veins.

Do we not know that we ourselves have failed?
Our valleys wide, our long green fields
We have bestrewn with our own dead.
In shop and mart we have befouled our souls.
Our corn is withered and our faces black
With smoke of hate.

We make the gesture and we go to die.
Had we been true to our own land our sweetness then had quite
    remade the world.
We now are true to failure grim—
We go in prayer to die.

To our own souls we take the killer's sin.
Into the waters black our souls we fling.
We take the chances of the broader dream.
Not ours but all the worlds—our fields.
We enter in.

Mid-American Chants, 1918

DIRGE OF WAR

It begins with little creeping pains that run across the breast. Good-bye,
brother. I see your arm is withered and your lusts are dead. I did not
think the end would come so soon. It has—good-bye.

In the night we remembered to believe in hell. Wide we threw the
window to behold the fog. Men stumbled in the darkness—a cry
arose—then came war.

Now, brother—let's ponder—say we draw apart. Woman come to
fatherhood and the world upset. My little naked soldiers are playing
on the floor. I strike and bid you go. If you go, all is gone.

There is a thing you must do—let's get back to that. You must strike
out alone, get out of this room. You must go upon your journey.
Don't stay here—now be gone—good-bye.

The gray and purple lesson of the night comes on. What we dare not
face must now come home to us. Hear the guns—dull—in the night.

Back of us our fathers—let that go. Don't confuse us here—alone—
with memories that can't stand—and run—in our night. I'll tell you
what I want—be still.

I want to creep and creep and lie face downward on the rim of hell. I
want your breathing body to be torn from me. I want hell and guns
to be stilled by the aching thrust of new things into life. I want death
perfect and new love achieved. I want much.

Believe it or not I actually did run in the dusty hallways of my own
life before this began. I went into the long empty halls, breathed the
stale dust of all old things.

I knew and yet I did not know. That's what I want to say—by song
and by the jarring note of song that cannot sing.

I was coming with America—dreaming with America—hoping with
America—then war came.

I'm an aching old thing and the dream come true. I am sick with my
last sickness here alone. I am creeping, creeping, creeping—in the
night—in the halls. I am death—I am war—I am hate.

And that's all, brother. I dare not hope. The childishness has left me.
I am dead. Over the fields a shriek—a cry. I pay my fare to hell—I
die—I die.

Mid-American Chants, 1918

A NEW TESTAMENT: I

It would be absurd for me to try writing of myself and then solemnly
to put my writings into print. I am too much occupied with myself
to do the thing well. I am like you in that regard. Although I think
of myself all the time I cannot bring myself to the conviction that
there is anything of importance attached to the life led by my
conscious self. What I want to say is this:—men may talk to me until
they are blind of the life force and of the soul that liveth beyond the
passing away of the husk called the body—

For me life centres in myself, in the hidden thing in myself. I am sorry my
flesh is not more beautiful, that I cannot live happily in contemplation
of myself and must of necessity turn inward to discover what is
interesting in the making of me. It would simplify things if I could
love my outward self and it must be the same with you.

There have been periods when I have almost succeeded in living alone
and forgetting my bodily life. They were interesting times. I will talk
to you of them. There was a period once, when I lived in a room
on the North Side in Chicago and came near achieving complete
happiness. The woman who managed the house was a slattern. She
did not keep the room clean so I cleaned it myself. I had a house
painter come and paint the walls and the woodwork a dull grey
to match the skies of my city. Twice a week I got on all fours and
wiped the floors with a wet cloth. Every evening, after I had dined, I
went into the room and locked the door.

My plan of having the walls and the woodwork painted a dull grey
to match the habitual grey of the skies of my city was entirely
successful. At dusk and even at night the walls and woodwork of my
room disappeared. To walk barefooted on the floor—going from my
bed toward the window—was an odd sensation. It was like walking
out of the window of a tall building into the sky, into the unknown.

The room I lived in at that time was in a building made of red brick,
black with grime, and my windows looked down into the city. I
suspect now that I was, for perhaps a year, what is called insane.

I bought me a heavy coat and sometimes on winter nights threw open the windows and curled up in a large chair, wide awake until morning. I must be very strong. I have in fact heard that all insane people are strong. In the morning I was as rested as though I had slept and went off to my daily work of making a living with no feeling of fatigue.

An experience such as I am talking about having had cannot be successfully achieved if you are physically nervous as most Americans are and as I am most of the time. When I was very tired I was not happy in my room and sometimes felt so out of place that I went off to spend the night at a hotel. The thing to be aimed at was to become very quiet so that the mind appeared to run out of the body. A sense of floating was at times achieved. One's mind reached out. It was at first like a small baby learning to crawl. Then later it was like a white bodied boy and ran over the roofs of houses. It comprehended the city of Chicago. It comprehended all cities.

There was a sense too of things in nature I had not known before. For one thing all women became pure. For the first time I found out that there cannot be such a thing as an impure man or woman. That was one of the first things my white boy mind discovered for me.

There was one woman I remember well. She lived in a room also painted grey. The point of the greyness of our two rooms was that the walls ceased to exist.

My white bodied mind ran over the tops of trees and into the house where the woman's body sat in the grey stillness. Her mind had also run away into the night. I did not touch her body—fearing it would be cold, as I am sure my body was cold—sitting alone in the room in the house on the North Side in Chicago.

I am striving to give you a sense of infinite things that have happened to me as I am sure they have happened also to you. We do not commune thus together often enough. I am afraid even as I begin to write, that my mood will not be strong or prolonged enough to carry me on to the things I want to speak of with a good deal of attention to detail.

You will see at once that the room on the North Side of Chicago and my life there has for the moment returned to me very vividly. That is because it has no reality. There are other things of which I hope to write that are more definite but if I remain true to my desires nothing in this book will be very definite. The book is itself, as you have by this time no doubt suspected, an effort to escape out of the house and the room of my life, to visit you the reader indefinitely, to touch with my thoughts your lips, your hair, your body that I trust will remain as cold as the body of the woman my boy mind visited. I am like everyone else who has in reverence put pen to paper, impatient with the limitations of pen and paper. If your body becomes warm as you read on and into my testament my mind will become excited and all will be destroyed.

I was in that grey room a long time, looking out at the city of Chicago and thinking of Illinois and Iowa. My room faced south and west so my mind went in those directions. It even visited Kentucky and Missouri although it did not go farther south, into the cotton growing states or into the southwest, into Texas.

In the room my mind grew more vigorous than myself as expressed in my body. There is however nothing uncanny in all this. If you think there is you are mistaken. We are all so hurried and harried through life that we forget the possibilities of life and are but too prone to take short cuts into the supernatural. Not many of us get, even for a few months during a long life, into a quiet place where the needs of our bodies become hushed and secondary. I have sometimes seen old sick people I thought were doing the thing of which I speak, but I could not be sure of them. It is my own persistent notion that one needs to be well, to be healthy and strong to achieve the delights of insanity, to live in other words outside the husk of oneself.

It will be understood between us that I am a man with fat cheeks, neither handsome or very homely, of the medium height. I go about the middle-western part of America making a living, visiting towns, seeing people. I eat food in restaurants, go to dine sometimes in houses, meet occasionally notably men who have got up in the world. Once in a long time someone writes of me, saying I am a notable man.

I know that is a lie. I know well enough there never has been, cannot be such a thing as a notable man.

I am however determined — for a curious reason it is not worthwhile to try to record — to attempt to reveal myself.

One of the motives back of my attempt — a somewhat obvious motive — is that I live in Chicago in a day when very little that is true concerning life comes to the surface. In a purely subconscious way I am a patriot. I live in a wide valley of cornfields and men and towns and strange jangling sounds, and in spite of the curious perversion of life here I have a feeling that the great basin of the Mississippi River, where I have always lived and moved about, is one day to be the seat of the culture of the universe. As I have talked with very few men from other places I have not found out whether they have or have not the same hallucination regarding their native lands. Anyway I have it regarding my own.

And I have another feeling. It seems to me that every man or woman who lives in my land in my time is as a seed planted. My mind has spent hours playing with the idea. I have elaborated it infinitely. The industrialism that has so crushed the spirits of the people of my day is, I say to myself, but the damp cold heavy earth lying over the seeds. We are in the winter of time. All seed must be planted and must lie in the damp and cold until warm days come.

I strike upon this seed motive now because I fancy it was born with the birth of my fanciful self. I cannot remember but I often tell myself it was born while I lived in the North Side room I have been talking to you about—the room you will have to make a special effort not to forget did not exist. I have a desire to make you sense me in that room and if you are to grow to care for me to make you care for me there, sitting wide awake on a winter night in my great coat and looking with blind eyes down in the heart of Mid-America.

I am sure I was a seed then and that you were a seed then and that we are both but seeds now. We are both buried deeply in life. We sometimes strive and strain, trying to escape our obvious fate. Vaguely also we try each to fertilize the spirits of the other.

It is unnecessary to try to carry the figure on but it is an almost sensual pleasure to me to think that perhaps I will fertilize your mind with my notion. That is my egotism. I think of you going along in Indianapolis or Chicago or Minneapolis thinking of the words I have put down. As the whole purpose of my writing is my own pleasure I will stop writing for the present and give myself over to the contemplation of you, for a moment and in a passing way, thinking the thought I have suggested to you.

The Little Review, 1919

The fancy comes to me that thoughts like layers of smoke are lying
along the street through which I have been walking. There are always
banks of smoke hanging in the streets of Chicago. There is a sensual
gratification to me in the notion that the crowds of men and women
who have just passed me and who have gone before me have also lost
themselves in the thoughts I have been lost in. By indirection I have
been making love to all the men and women of a city.

To be sure there are degrees to the experience I have been unconsciously
having. All men and women are not equally susceptible.

I am one who has no yesterday and grope dreamily toward a
tomorrow. I am like you. You are not at all the thing you have so
foolishly imagined yourself to be. But I will not set myself up to
define you. I am nothing. I believe nothing. I would like to walk
with you. If possible I would like to imagine you beautiful while
you are in my presence. By indirection I wish to caress you, to touch
with soft fingers the lids of your eyes, to lie like a gem in the hollow
of your hand. For the moment that is the height of my desire.

Many people have walked before me in the street, having as I have
declared had a sort of intercourse with me. As I walk with you I
will tell you of them. Before me, in the forefront of my fancy, went
a trembling old man. Ahead of him was a glorious woman, full
breasted, strong at the shoulders. The wind blew her skirts and I saw
that her legs were shapely and strong. She did not know that I knew
what she was thinking about.

At the risk of being impertinent I will remind you again that this is an
experience I have not had. When we are better acquainted I will quit
harping on my insanity, my love of God and the other traits of my
character.

Before the old man and the strong beautiful woman went many others
in the canyon of the street. They walked like myself under the
smoke pall of Chicago and like myself they walked in and out of the

layers of thought. They were all like myself fanciful folk. They were making—each of them—designs in the darkness. In the dark street they felt for the threads of life with the fingers of their hands.

How very many people going in and out of the thoughts. I fancied that I found a blank, a vacant place. Some brash impertinence out of my conscious life made me want to attempt to fill the blank.

"I will put in this blank place a thought, a thought of my own," I said. It will be passed through by men, women and children. I crept into a doorway and watched, hoping childishly that the whole rhythm of the universe would be changed by my act.

Nothing happened of course, I suspect because my act was more than half conscious. My thought had no strength of its own. The wind blew it away.

The streets of Chicago are roaring whirling places. Shrill human cries run like brightly colored threads through the thoughts of every man and woman who walks abroad. It is very foolish to try to be definite as I was as I attempted to lay down the thought. Nothing is to be achieved by being smart and definite, and to be vague—they keep telling me—is to be insane, a little unbalanced.

In a plow factory, on the West Side in Chicago, there are great tanks in the floor. The tanks are kept filled with many colored liquids. By machinery plows are lifted from the factory floor and swung above the tanks. They are dipped and become instantly and completely black, red, brown, purple, blue, grey, pink.

Can a plow be pink? I have the trick of thinking too rapidly in color. I cannot remember the color of the eyes of my sister. The color of the cheeks of my mistress I cannot remember.

An endless clanking goes on in my head. It is the machinery of the life in which I hang suspended. I and all the men and women in the streets are at this moment being dipped anew in the life of Chicago. There is no yesterday for any of us. We hang by a hook in the present. Whatever lies behind this second of conscious time is a lie and I have set myself to lie to the limit. By my lying and by that road only will I succeed in expressing something of the truth of the life into which I also have been flung.

This is evidently true. Plows may not be pink but the prevailing color of the flesh of people is pink. We have all been dipped in a dawn.

Had I not been betrayed by my egotism into trying to fill the blank space in the thought layers in the street my whole life might have been different. But for my act I might have found in the fancy that had come to me the rhythm of my age and got fame like a great man.

I am instead a man of infinite littleness, a maker of words. The gratification to me is that I am so much like you. That is why I understand and love you. I will not however attempt to become your lover. There is destruction in that and we are a long way from being fit to destroy each other. If however we find as we go along that your insanity strikes the same chord as my own something remarkable may happen.

The Little Review, 1919

UNTITLED

Your whole life is like the dark hallways of a great house late at night when there are no lights. You are one of many great houses I have visited. Russia is a house and so are you. China is an old house. Many old houses have fallen down.

For a long time I had the illusion I was helping to build a new house in which you and I were to live. A wind has blown the illusion away. Building is going on but I have nothing to do with it. It may be that you are the builder.

I am perplexed with trying to find out who does the building. I creep in the dusty hallways and hear many strange voices. The voices of men and women resound out of the darkness.

The voices cry out to me that they are the voices of builders but as I go forward, feeling with my hands on the walls, I do not come to the place of the building.

A soft voice has whispered to me that there is no such thing as a builder. It was a woman's voice. "The noise you hear is made by heavy untruths in the hands of arrogant men," she said. "The men lean out at a window. They beat on a brazen sky. They are trying to make holes in the sky."

I suspect the soft voice expressed also a hunger. It came from a woman I met in the darkness. I had at the moment been running desperately in the dark hallways of my house, in the house into which I was dropped at the beginning of life. I am blind and when I run I knock against things. I knocked against her.

My body had become warm from the running. The woman may also have been blind. Our warm bodies touched in the darkness. For a long time we stood close together in silence and darkness. There was a drumming in my head.

All noises ceased, even the perpetual noise made by those who call themselves builders. In the darkness I fancied I heard the scream of an animal . . .

Later it was quiet again and I heard only the voice. It spoke softly and told again of the false builders and of the heavy untruths with which they beat on the brazen sky.

I shall remember the voice telling its beautiful lie as long as I live.

The woman and I shall never find each other again.

There are too many hallways in the houses.

My house is filled with the smell of new-cut logs and the walls are rough with the marks of the trowels of builders.

My house is noisy with the clangor of hammers.

I shall never escape out of my house.

When the time comes I shall take an untruth into my hands and lean out at the window to beat on the sky.

Section seven from "A New Testament: III,"
The Little Review, 1919

UNTITLED

When I stop stretching my mind it slips back and lies dead and lifeless
    like the rubberband of a boy's slingshot. For hours and days it lies
    dead and meaningless like a wornout shoe thrown into an alleyway
    in a city.

A dirty boy with a twisted shoulder has thrown me over a fence and
    I fall rattling on stone steps at the back of a house where lives a
    woman whose lover I once was. Once I kissed the woman when
    we had both been drinking wine. It was late at night and there was
    snow on the ground. Her cheeks were cold but her lips were warm.
    Her father owned a factory where the shoes are made. The father of
    the crippled boy worked at a bench in the factory.

Section one from "A New Testament: IV,"
The Little Review, 1920

UNTITLED

Everything I have found out about life is common knowledge. The dogs in the street bark my knowledge in the dark nights. Two cats live in an alleyway back of a gloomy building where I have a hole in which to sleep and where for long hours I lie awake, thinking, dreaming, putting up my hands in the darkness, whispering your name and the names of other beautiful things I have seen.

This is in the deep quiet of the night when you have passed into a dreamless sleep. This is when the smoke of the city has been blown away. The wind has lifted the smoke off the city as an old factory hand homeward bound on a winter evening might lift a dirty carpet off the form of a dead child he has found lying in an alleyway.

From section two of "A New Testament: IV,"
The Little Review, 1920*

---

*Section two of Anderson's poem "A New Testament: IV" is made up of five parts: The first two parts are presented as "Untitled" (from section two of "A New Testament: IV") in this volume. The last three parts were selected by Anderson to appear in his book *A New Testament* as "In a Workingman's Rooming House," which is included in this volume under that title.

You have grey eyes very large and round. Your eyes are like moons rising out of a swamp in November. Your eyes are like the eyes of little foxes.

Your eyes are grey. Tomorrow they shall be red with weeping, as red as a sumac growing beside a dusty road in Ohio. The feet of many people are running over the grey of your eyes.

It is my passion to run like a frightened little animal over the grey of your eyes. My own story is curious.

Long ago I emerged from a hole in the valley where a stream of water runs down over rocks. I crept out through the hole to a flat black rock and lay sprawling. I stared at the sun. On all sides of me lay the forests. I went back into the hole naked and came out again on all fours with long hair on my body.

It was ordained I could not live among men.

Because I was naked and ashamed I started to crawl away into the North. The hunger that has never been appeased lay deep in me. It is because of my hunger that I have learned to walk standing up, that I have learned to walk up and down.

It is because of my hunger I am standing on a yellow place making marks in the sand at the edge of a stream.

My place for sand writing is narrow and I write with a dull stick that makes the words crudely. There are many words I do not know. I have missed many sweet words.

I am a young man in the flush of my passions.
I am an old grey man with brittle bones.
I am on yellow sand by a stream at dawn.
The hair is worn from my body because I have been crawling on my belly through towns.

If my sand place were large and long I should be able to tell you a
    wonderful tale.

The water will arise in the stream and wash my story away.
The hair is worn from my body from crawling through towns.
I am a dumb man crept out of a hole in the hills.

I have no words.
The stick with which I write is dull.
I have no words.
My stick is worn away.

I wonder why your grey eyes did not come with the dawn and teach
    me the words. I was for a long time alone and dumb.

There was no word for the whispering wind.
There was no word for the groaning of trees.
There was no word for the false dawn that looked over the tops of the trees.

The light of the true dawn made music among the trees. Why were
    you not there? Why did you not give me the words? You were in
    the towns when I crept on my belly like a beast. You had made the
    towns and they lay on broad plains between hills. On the street of
    a town there was a woman with black hair. She did not have grey
    eyes. Was she your sister? She was clothed in a black garment and
    ran screaming through streets. Many men were tied to posts beneath
    the eaves of the houses. Icicles made from the tears of children hung
    from the houses. The icicles clung to the eaves of the houses.

It was night when I crept into the towns. As I went forward, creeping
    like a cat on my belly, the men trembled like leaves in a forest God
    has touched with his fingers.

Something occurred. A warm wave of feeling ran up through the men.
    It ascended to the eaves of the houses. Drops of icy cold water fell
    on the heads of the men.

The men were very cold.
The woman with black hair, clad in a black garment, ran past me
    through the streets.
She screamed.

I did not learn any new sweet word in the town but I learned to scream
    like a woman in pain.

The Little Review, 1920

A NEW TESTAMENT: X

I have no words with which to tell you where I have been since I saw
you last.

Now I am back at the yellow place by the sand reach.

A hand reached up out of the ground before me and lifted the lids of
my eyes.

I have become an old man with small brittle bones.
The chill of many dawns is in the hair of my head.
The sandy place where I have taken a fancy to write words with a dull
stick is cut and crossed with yellow streaks.
There has been a flood.
The waters have been my friend—they have run over the sand, wiping
my words away.
The words have escaped into the grass.
I shall never find the lost words.

There was a word whose legs became black. He danced drearily back
and forth on the sand and screamed like a woman in travail. I should
have forgotten the screaming of women but for the dancing word.

It was night and I went into the mountains. Then I remembered that
the valley of the Mississippi River is a flat place between the breasts
of my mother. That realization gave me unspeakable joy. My
mother's head lies far to the north in a grey silence.
I have climbed upon the nipple of one of my mother's breasts.

Since I was here, in the days you have forgotten, I have come into the
wonder of sight.

* * *

It is morning and a hush had come over the valley. I am weary but that
is of no importance. Do not shake the branches of the grass as I
speak to you of my adventure.

The millions of men and women who live in the valley of the
Mississippi River had run out into the plains. That was at the
beginning of evening. They had come—running swiftly—into a
close place—into the center of a bowl. All men and all women
and children were there—they had come out of the towns—out of
cities—out of alleyways in the cities—out of houses in towns.

Farmers had quit milking cows to come into the plains. They had given
over the planting and the raking of fields. Men had come running
out at the door-ways of factories. Women with hanging heads and
stooped shoulders had come.

Children had come laughing but had stopped laughing to stand quietly
in the crowd, understanding more than their elders.

Everyone stood quite still.

It was time for my word to be heard.

I sat on the nipple of my mother's breast and looked out over the plains.

I tried to say the word but my tongue became dry and hard like a
stone. "Now," I thought, "the word that has never come to me will
find lodgment on my lips. There will come a word out of the cellar
of my being. My word will rise slowly—creeping toward my tongue
and my lips. My word will rattle and reverberate along the rafters of
my being."

Nothing happened at all. On the vast plains there was only a tense
silence. I came down from my high place—down from the nipple of
my mother's breast.

I went within myself as a tired man at evening might go in at the door
of his house. Inside myself all was silence. Dust sifted down through
the room of my house. My dead tongue was a stone rolled against
the doorway of myself. I took the stone in my hand and threw it
away—out through a window.

* * *

On the vast plains of the Mississippi Valley an army is standing.
It has said no word.
No word has been said to it.
The army is silent.
It is a host without numbers.
It is a host without banners.
It is a naked host that has staring eyes.
It is a host that stands still.

* * *

No winds blow on the plains. I have just come from there and it is
    evening and quiet. Silently stands the host, staring with calm eyes
    into the North. I will take you there if to go falls within the province
    of your desires. You also shall sit upon the nipple of my mother's
    breast and look out over the host. You shall sit beside me while
    night and the shadows of death play over the host.
You shall look into my mother's eyes.
Far into the North you shall look.
The eyes of my mother are open.
They are like a sea filled with salt.
Shadows flit over the balls of their eyes.
The little shadows of men chase each other over the quiet eyes of my
    mother that are hidden away in the silence—far to the North.
Do not shake the branches of the grass as I speak to you of my
    adventure.
Your eyes are very grey and large and round.
I have come down from the nipple of my mother's breast.
I write with a blunt stick in the sand at the edge of the flowing waters.
I shall run on many nights through the towns.
I shall run on many nights through the cities.
I shall run on many nights through the alleyways of the cities.

The Little Review, 1920

UNTITLED

It is my own belief that the whole plan was matured in advance.
It is my own belief I took hold of insanity as, in a crowded city street,
  one takes hold of the hand of a child.
The incident, however, may have had more significance than that.
Insanity is a slow moving liquid poured into a cup.
As you look into the cup your eyes change their color.
The liquid is green.
It is an ultimate blue.
The liquid is colorless.
It moves out of the West into the East.

Section four from "A New Testament: XII,"
The Little Review, 1920

UNTITLED

Did you ever have a notion of this kind?—there is an orange, or say an apple, lying on a table before you. You put out your hand to take it. Perhaps you eat it, make it a part of your physical life. Have you touched? Have you eaten? That's what I wonder about.

The whole subject is only important to me because I want the apple. What subtle flavours are concealed in it—how does it taste, smell, feel? Heavens, man, the way the apple feels in the hand is something—isn't it?

For a long time I thought only of eating the apple. Then later its fragrance became something of importance, too. The fragrance stole out through my room, through a window and into the streets. It made itself a part of all the smells of the streets. The devil!—in Chicago or Pittsburgh, Youngstown or Cleveland it would have had a rough time.

That doesn't matter.

The point is that after the form of the apple began to take my eye I often found myself unable to touch at all. My hands went toward the object of my desire and then came back.

There I sat, in the room with the apple before me, and hours passed. I had pushed myself off into a world where nothing has any existence. Had I done that, or had I merely stepped, for the moment, out of the world of darkness into the light?

It may be that my eyes are blind and that I cannot see.

It may be I am deaf.

My hands are nervous and tremble. How much do they tremble? Now, alas! I am absorbed in looking at my own hands.

With these nervous and uncertain hands may I really feel for the form of things concealed in the darkness?

Forward to *Horses and Men*, 1924

UNTITLED

While you can see me you shall not have me.

While you can reach out your hand and touch my fingers you shall not
know I am alive.

In the time of my death and decay life shall come out of me and flow
into you.

Epigraph to A New Testament, 1927

ONE WHO LOOKED UP AT THE SKY

It would be strange if, by a thought, a man could make Illinois
   pregnant.

It would be strange if the man who just left my house and went
   tramping off in the darkness to take a train to a distant place came
   here from a far place, came over lands and seas, to impregnate me.

A New Testament, 1927

A YOUNG MAN

At times, just for a moment I am a Caesar, a Napoleon, an Alexander.
 I tell you it is true.

If you men who are my friends and those of you who are
 acquaintances could surrender yourselves to me for just a little
 while.

I tell you what—I would take you within myself and carry you around
 within me as though I were a pregnant woman.

There is a testament out of life to the man who has just left my presence.
 There is a testament to be made to a woman who once held me in her
 arms and who got no child. There is a testament to be made to this
 house, to the sunshine that falls on me, to these legs of mine clad in
 torn trousers, to the sea and to a city sleeping on a prairie.

A New Testament, 1927

SONG NUMBER ONE

My life has passed into a coma of waiting but I wait no more intelligently
    than you. Sometimes as I walk in the streets a look of intelligence comes
    into my eyes. If I had not watched closely the eyes of my brothers I
    would be often deceived by what I see in my own eyes.

It is only by going about in secret I can stumble into the pathway of truth.
    When truth has passed through the streets of a town or has walked
    on wet leaves in a forest there is a faint smell. It is blown about by the
    wind. I smell the footsteps of truth but I do not walk in the footsteps.

I have recently thrown out of my arms the maiden placed there by my
    father—a liar.
I sit in a stone chair in a cold place.
I am beset by many pains.
Pain comes running to me out of the bodies of men and women.
I am bred out of the lusts of the world.
I am become the abiding place of little lustful thoughts that weave in
    and out of the minds of my people.

It is only to comfort my solitude I whisper to myself it is thus the new man
    emerges. It is a thought to play with, a ball to bounce off the wall. I
    have whispered to myself that the new man emerges out of the womb
    of an engine, that his birth cry arises out of a clangor of sounds.
My thoughts are tossed back and forth on a wall.
As you sit with me you shall be compelled to share my fate.
All you who live in the valley have had sticks thrust into your eyes.
You are shepherds of blind sheep.
You shall sit in the chair of stone.
You shall sit in the narrow place.
You shall be pregnant.
You shall sit in the stone chair at night and the throbbing of iron cities
    shall be in the intricate veins of your being.
There are walls of stone.
There are walls faced with iron.
Between them you shall sit.

The little tricks of my mind shall explain nothing to you. If I should
dig myself a grave and bury myself by the light of a summer moon
you would pass like a flitting shadow along the further side of the
wall.

It is, however, my desire to die in the midst of a more intelligent pain.
My desire is as yet no more than a tiny white worm that lives under
a sidewalk in an Illinois town.

You shall not know my desire until you slip into my place in the chair.
The noises of the world are tremendous.
The walls of the cities throb.
There is a new song stuck in the brazen throats of the cities.
There is an American song.
There is a song nobody knows.

There is a child born of an engine in a bed of stone. American cities are
pregnant. You understand what I mean. My insanity is crystal-clear
to you as you sit in the chair of stone. To you my insanity is a white
streak of moonlight that falls across the smoke-begrimed streets of
your city.

My insanity is a slow creeping vine clinging to a wall.
My insanity is a white worm with a fire in its forehead.

* * *

I write only to beguile the hours of the waiting. It is that I am
whispering about. I have put my lusts into an iron cage at the side of
the chair. I am watching the people who file up out of the valley to
go like wavering shadows along the face of the wall.
I sit patiently watching the small white thing that comes out of my
body to creep on the face of the wall.

A New Testament, 1927

SONG NUMBER FOUR

You are a child who sleeps and throws his hands up over his head.
You are a strong man who walks in a street at night. In the silence you
    hear little sounds.
You are a country girl and live in Nebraska. At evening you drive cows
    along a lane to your father's barn.

* * *

I grope my way toward you in the darkness.
I feel my way along the face of a wall.
I gather little stones and lay them along the face of the wall.

* * *

You are an old woman without teeth.
In the stairway of an old building you sit. You whine at me.
Why do you not arise and sing? Why do you not make a testament to me?

* * *

You have forgotten that I crawled into your arms as you lay in a bed.
    You have forgotten that we walked in an orchard.

* * *

You are very lame. You have a twisted foot. It is your occupation to sell
    newspapers in the street before a railroad station. Your fingers have
    become like fruit that has been lying a long time in the sun. Your
    voice testifies in the city. You cry aloud in the city.

How gentle you were that time when together we saw the little
    shadows playing on the face of the wall. Do you remember how the
    tears ran out of your eyes?

* * *

You are a small man sitting in a dark room in the early morning. Look, you have killed a woman. Her body lies on the floor. Your face is white and your hands tremble. A testament is creeping from between your teeth. It makes your teeth chatter.

You are a young man in the schools.

You walk up the face of a hill.

You are an insane driver of sheep.

You are a woman in a brown coat, a fish merchant in a village, a man who throws coal in at the mouth of a furnace, a maiden who presses the body of her lover against the face of the wall.

You are a bush.

You are a wind.

You are the gun of a soldier.

You are the hide that has been drawn over the face of a drum.

You are a young birch tree swaying in a wind.

You are one who has been slain by a falling tree in a forest.

Your body has been destroyed by a flying mass of iron in the midst of a battle.

Your voice comes up out of a great confusion.

Listen, little lost one, I am testifying to you as I creep along the face of a wall.

I am making a testament as I gather stones and lay them along the face of a wall.

A New Testament, 1927

HUNGER

On farms the dogs bark and old women groan as they crawl into beds. The scraping feet of old men make a shuffling sound on the floors.

In the cities the street cars rattle and bang. The motors make great moving rivers in streets.

It is winter now but in the spring there will be flowers in the fields and at the edge of roadsides. The spring rains will wash thoughts away. There will be long-stemmed flowers reaching up from shaded places under the trees.

I am no more true than yourself, no more alive than yourself.

You are a man and I would take hold of your hand. You are a woman, I would embrace you. You are a child, I would be unashamed to stand in your presence. The flower that is myself has a long stem.

A New Testament, 1927

DEATH

I do not belong to the company of those who wear velvet gowns and look at the stars. God has not taken me into his house to sit with him. When his house has burned bright with lights I have stayed in the streets.

My desire is not to ascend but to go down. My soul does not hunger to float. I do not wish to pass out of the animal kingdom and into the kingdom of birds, to fold my wings and pitch into the arms of a wind that blows in from the sea. The voice of the wind does not call to me.

When I am strong and the noise of the cities roars in my ears it is my desire to be a little mole that works under the ground. I would creep beneath the roots of the grass.
I would go under the foundations of buildings.
I would creep like a drop of rain along the far, hair-like roots of a tree.

When springs come and strength surges into my body I would creep beneath the roots of grasses far out into the fields.
I would go under the fields that are plowed.
I would creep down under the black fields. I would go softly, touching and feeling my way.

I would be little brother to a kernel of corn that is to feed the bodies of men.

A New Testament, 1927

THE HEALER

My body does not belong to me.
My body belongs to tired women who have found no lovers.
It belongs to half men and half women.
My body belongs to those who lust and those who shrink from lusting.
My body belongs to the roots of trees.
It shall be consumed with fire on a far horizon.
The smoke that arises from my burning body shall make the western
  skies golden.
My body belongs to a Virginia mob that runs to kill negroes. It belongs
  to a woman whose husband was killed in a railroad wreck. It
  belongs to an old man dying by a fire in a wood, to a negress who
  is on her knees scrubbing floors, to a millionaire who drives an
  automobile.
My body belongs to one whose son has killed a man and has been sent
  to a prison. It belongs to those who have the lust for killing and to
  those who kill.
My body is a stick a strong man has stuck in the ground. It is a post a
  drunkard has leaned against.
My body is a cunning wind. It is a thought in the night, a wound that
  bleeds, the breath of a god, the quavering end of a song.

A New Testament, 1927

MAN SPEAKING TO A WOMAN

You have come to me from a tall awkward city. You have come to me
   from the sister cities of the north. On your way here to me you have
   run in and out of a thousand cities that lie like unhatched eggs on
   the prairies.

You are a distraught woman with tangled hair and once you owned a
   house in a street where wagons and motor trucks went up and down.
I am glad you are tangled in a web of thought.
I am glad your thoughts have driven you out of the cities.
You have come up a hill to a place where I sit.
I am glad.
I will take the end of a thought in my hand and walk back and forth.
I will climb into trees.
I will run in holes under the ground.
I will weave a web over yourself.

You shall sit on a stone under a wall where a gateway leads into the
   valley of truth and as I weave you into oblivion I will tell you a tale.

Long ago, on a day in October, a woman like you came here to the
   face of the wall. The shadow of many perplexities lay like a film
   over her eyes. She sat on the stone with her back to the wall as you
   sit now. My father, who was then a young man, laid long threads of
   thought over her body.
A stone fell out of the wall and the woman was killed.
The wall is strong but a stone fell out of the wall.
It made a great noise.
A noise like the firing of guns was heard to the North and the South.

In the Valley there was a day set aside for the cleansing of doorsteps.
The sound of the tinkling of bells came over the wall.
A stone fell out of the wall on the head of a woman.
She fled from my father.
She fled like a frightened bird over the wall.

A New Testament, 1927

TESTAMENT OF AN OLD MAN

I am an old man sitting in the sun before the door of my house. The
wind blows sharply, shaking golden leaves off the trees. It is late
October and cold but I am not cold. My house protects me. The
fingers of the wind cannot find me. The sun plays gently over
my body. The dying fires within me are a little stirred. The blood
mounts up through my body into my brain. My brain is fed with
warm blood. It awakens.

King David, when he was old, could not be warmed by the virgins
lying with him in a bed but I am warmed by the soft kiss of the sun.
The sun is my sweetheart. There is nothing in the world so fair as
the sun. The sun is my virgin. The virgins that were brought to King
David in old times looked at him and the blood did not mount into
their bodies. They lay in bed with the King but they did not warm
him. There was no warmth in them. My virgin, the sun, comes very
close. She takes me into her arms. She warms me. The body of the
sun is pressed close to my body. The sun's breath, fragrant with
love, warms me.

My brain that has been for many days asleep, runs madly. It runs down
across plains. My brain is a hound that has come out of its kennel.
It runs with long strides, swiftly, like a shadow. It runs as a shadow
runs, swiftly, o'er wheat and corn fields, o'er towns and cities, o'er
seas.

My awakened brain is a hound dog come out of its kennel. It is a
hound dog, white and silent and swift.

My brain runs backward and forward, it runs on into cities the
foundations of which have never been laid, it runs o'er fields that
shall be planted at the hands of men not yet come from the womb,
not conceived yet.

My hound brain is a whispering wind. It runs backward and forward.
It runs into new lives. It runs back into old lives.

It has run beside Jesus the Prince as he walked alone on a mountain. It has lain all night at the door of a tent where Caesar was encamped on a hillside in Gaul.

My hound mind lay whining all night at the feet of the Caesar. We ran out of the camp. We ran into cities. We ran to where Caesar's wife lay in a bed. As Caesar slept we groveled and fought with other dogs in the street of the mighty city of Rome.

My hound mind has seen cities rise out of the plains and it has seen cities destroyed. It has seen tall oaks grow, mature and decay where Ruth went to glean in the harvest. It once lived in a slave who carried great stones to build a cathedral to the glory of God.

My hound first came into my body when I was a lad tramping in the fields. It went with me to live in the towns. Through a long life it has stayed in its kennel but now it is fleeing away.

Look how it runs. O'er towns and cities it runs. It runs like a shadow o'er the seas. Someday it will not return to its kennel. My old body, now warmed by the sun, shall be put under ground. Old words will be said. Quivering voices shall sing quivering songs. My hound shall sit on its haunches and look. It shall forget and later remember.

The sun has warmed me. I call my hound back to me over the plains. I caress it. My voice is raised in a song. My house shakes with my cries. I spread banners afar, over the sky.

My hound mind has brought me the love of the old. It has brought me the love of the lust. It has made me a proud man who walks on the bodies of slaves. It has taught me the lust of the purple robe, the lust of the lovely bodies of women.

Who knew as I walked among men how I lusted, what gold coins dripped from my fingers, how my blood was hot with the lust of war, of killing, of glory.

Who knew that I was a king walking the streets of a factory town, begging for bread, sleeping in straw.

With my hound asleep in its kennel I walked with a Caesar. I played at battles with a Corsican corporal.

I lived in a factory town. I lived in the palace and walked in the park of a king.

Who knew that I made beautiful American cities. Who knew I planted purple and gold flowers on the ash heaps of cities.

Who knew how my soul knelt to the beauty of lives. Who knew how I knelt before lives, how like a white Christ I hungered and loved my way into lives.

My hound mind has been into the mountains with Jesus. It has been with the gentle Confucius. It has been with all gentle men.

It has been with the mighty and proud. It has been with those who slew in the darkness and threw the knife into a bush. It has been with those who stole money at night, with a boy who crept into a barn lusting alone, with a woman who opened softly the door to look for her lover.

I am a man who sits in the sun before the door of his house. My body grows old. The hinges creak on the door of the kennel. My hound mind runs out over the plains. It runs backward and forward. It has run back into lives. It runs on into new lives.

King David could not be warmed by the virgins that crept with him into a bed but my sweetheart the sun has brought warmth into my body.

I shall call my hound back to me over the plains. I shall caress it. My voice shall be raised in a song. My house shall shake with my cries. I shall spread banners afar over the skies.

A New Testament, 1927

HALF-GODS

The little half-gods are whining in the street. The strong medicine of
life has burned their bellies and their skins are wrinkled. Their bones
have become brittle and their voices weak. They are too cold and
too young. Words without meaning drop from their lips.

In the attempt to walk on the rim of life the half-gods have made
themselves engines of steel. The air is befouled. The children of men
choke in the streets.

My ears are befouled. I have a disease from sitting with half-gods in a
room. My clothes are befouled by the stench of the engines.

A New Testament, 1927

IN A WORKINGMAN'S ROOMING HOUSE

At two o'clock at night a steamboat whistle blows in the Chicago
River. A man who lives above me gets out of bed and goes
barefooted across the floor. His feet fall on the boards like the
fingers of a player on a silent piano filled with broken strings.

He strikes a match. I know what he is doing. He is lighting a candle in
order that God may see into his room and remember him in the time
of his death.

I do not arise and light a candle for the sake of God. I lie still and
think. God has multiplied himself so often in my sight that I cannot
see him by the light of a candle.

A New Testament, 1927

THOUGHTS OF A MAN PASSED IN A LONELY STREET AT NIGHT

I have gone to walk up and down. It is night and cold. I want to creep into you. You have made me by thinking of me and I declare you should be ashamed of what you have done.

Why have you not made me more pure? Why have you not made me more beautiful?

Your conception of me makes me a little ill. It forces me to run away from you into a field of fancy, into a forest of doubt. If I cannot be one who when weary lies in warm human layers of thought I shall become for the nonce and until I am rested something not human. I have passed out of your presence.

I will multiply myself until I pass like a vapor out of your mind.

I am a thing hung suspended in life.

There is no life in me, only a desire to creep into your arms and sleep after my long walking up and down.

A New Testament, 1927

ONE WHO SOUGHT KNOWLEDGE

There are just as many things to be found out as anyone knows. No one I have ever met or talked with knows very much.

Books are not such great things and most writers of books are fools. Believe me that is true. How many books I have read. How many singers I have gone to hear sing. How many times I have gone to galleries to see what paintings painters have painted.

Life has not advanced very far. We do not need to be afraid we will be late to the battle.

A New Testament, 1927

THE MINISTER OF GOD

It was on my knees at prayer in a quiet dark place when lust for
women came to me.

A New Testament, 1927

A PERSISTENT LOVER

It is early morning and you and I have shaken the sleep out of our
  bodies and renewed our covenant. We have struck with the flat part
  of our hands the face of the wall. We have bowed our heads in the
  midst of a cloud of vapor. By the strength of our understanding and
  by that alone we now stand on our feet.

We stand upon our feet in the midst of the waters.

The hillside and green stretches of country, that yesterday seemed
  to draw near, have receded out of our sight. In our place the grey
  surface of the waters runs in little ridges, changing color a little as
  the years pass and the days pass.

The waters go on. In their never ending movement the waters achieve
  the insanity we seek in vain. There is a persistent roaring noise,
  but the waters do not break upon the rocks. In the air above our
  heads sound breaks against sound. The hammering voices have
  not stopped since the forgotten dawn long ago when I found you
  standing alone.

In the morning at the break of dawn there is a moment of quiet. The
  noises do not cease but there is quiet.

In the evening when the day runs like a frightened rabbit into the hole
  of night there is quiet.

It would be a comfort to me to know that at this moment at the
  beginning of our day our minds run together.

It would be a comfort to me to know that as your mind runs like a
  tardy streak of light at the heels of night my mind also runs.

It would be a joy to me to know that our two minds plunge forward
  together into the receding distance, over the waters.

In my perplexity I lift my foot out of the firm sand at the bottom of the
river and then set it slowly down.
My head rocks from side to side.
My hands are like branches of trees.
My hands are like the mottled backs of poplar trees that stand upright
in a snowstorm that blows down a hill.

I look at my hands and think of minute physical things concerning
myself because I am loath to begin again thinking of you.
When I lift my eyes the day will be here.
I will see the wet strands of hair falling across your breasts.
Your tired eyes will look into mine.

The uselessness of all effort will be indicated by the droop of your
shoulders.
An impulse toward love will tighten the cords of my throat.

I will note again the nakedness of you, the smallness of the trunk
of your body, the way the corners of your mouth twitch with
weariness.

The lids of your eyes are always very heavy and grey in the shifting
light at the beginning of a day.

How would it be with me if I could ride like a passenger on the back
of your mind.

When I have tried we both sank out of sight under the waters.

Your mind should have been a boat in which we could lie together,
sleeping and resting, but I am afraid then I should have become truly
insane and run away in the night.

It has not gone well with us as we walked, going ever more and more
slowly forward into the drifting current of days. We have walked

too long on the face of the waters. More than once I have kept silent when I wanted to thrust you away, out of my sight.

Had I raised my hand to strike, our two hands would have met in the air above the waters.

There would have been a more and more terrible hammering of sound against sound.

Had I raised my hand to strike, my hand would have met your hand also intent upon striking.

You have hidden yourself from me with lovely assurance.

I did not want to know the thoughts that came to you in the midst of the day.

I wanted your thoughts put away.

Your legs have grown blue and as we stand in the waters my own legs have grown brittle.
The dawn has come.

The hammering of sound against sound begins in the air over our heads.

I raise my eyes to your eyes.
In a moment perhaps words will come to my lips.
In a moment, my beloved, I shall tell you anew the story of how, in a grey dawn long ago, I found you standing alone.

A New Testament, 1927

THE DUMB MAN

There is a story. I cannot tell it. I have no words. The story is almost forgotten but sometimes I remember.

The story concerns three men in a house in a street. If I could say the words I would sing the story. I would whisper it into the ears of women, of mothers. I would run through the world saying it over and over. My tongue would be torn loose. It would rattle against my lips.

The three men are in a room in a house. One is young and dandified. He continually laughs.

There is a second man who has a long white beard. He is consumed with doubt but occasionally his doubt leaves him and he sleeps.

A third man there is who has wicked eyes and who moves nervously about the room rubbing his hands together.

The three men are waiting, waiting.

Upstairs in the house there is a woman standing with her back to a wall, in half darkness by a window.

That is the foundation of the story. Everything I will ever know is distilled in it.

I remember a fourth man came to the house, a white silent man. Everything was as silent as the sea at night. His feet on the stone floor of the room where the three men were made no sound.

The man with wicked eyes became like a boiling liquid. He ran back and forth like a caged animal. The old grey man was infected by his nervousness. He kept pulling at his beard.

The fourth man, the white one, went upstairs to the woman.

There she was—waiting.

How silent the house was. How loudly all the clocks in the neighborhood ticked.

The woman upstairs craved love. That must have been the story. She hungered for love with her whole being. She wanted to create in love. When the white silent man came into her presence she sprang forward. Her lips were parted. There was a smile on her lips.

The white one said nothing. In his eyes there was no rebuke, no question. His eyes were as impersonal as stars.

Downstairs the wicked one whined and ran back and forth like a little lost hungry dog. The grey one tried to follow him about but presently grew tired and lay down on the floor to sleep. He never awoke again.

The dandified fellow lay on he floor too. He laughed and played with his tiny black mustache.

I have no words to tell what happened in my story. I cannot tell the story.

The white silent one may have been death.

The waiting eager woman may have been life.

Both the grey bearded man and the wicked one puzzle me. I think and think but do not understand them. Most of the time I do not think of them at all.

I keep thinking about the dandified man who laughed all through my story. If I could understand him I could understand everything. I could run through the world telling a wonderful story. I would no longer be dumb.

Why was I not given words? Why was I not given a mind? Why am I dumb? I have a wonderful story to tell but know no way to tell it.

A New Testament, 1927

A YOUNG JEW

Years and a life of it,
Sitting in a room,
Walking with my father in a street,
Hungering,
Hating,
Burning my flame out in an empty place.
The smoke from burning bodies goes straight up.
Fire everywhere.
My world is choked with smoke of burning men,
With smoldering fumes of fires,
With smoke of burning men.
My mother's breasts are tipped with flames.
She has suckled men in fire.
She has suckled me in flames.
Her breasts are tipped with flames.
My mother's eyes look out at burning men.
My father's eyes look back at old things burned and charred.
They are hungering in the streets,
Their eyes are tipped with flames,
Their eyes flee from their bodies, hungering in the streets.

A New Testament, 1927

THE STORY TELLER

Tales are people who sit on the doorstep of the house of my mind.
It is cold outside and they sit waiting.
I look out at a window.
The tales have cold hands.
Their hands are freezing.
A short thickly-built tale arises and threshes his arms about.
His nose is red and he has two gold teeth.

There is an old female tale sits hunched up in a cloak.

Many tales come to sit for a moment on the doorstep and then go away.
It is too cold for them outside.
The street before the door of the house of my mind is filled with tales.
They murmur and cry out, they are dying of cold and hunger.

I am a helpless man—my hands tremble.
I should be sitting on a bench like a tailor.
I should be weaving warm cloth out of the threads of thought.
The tales should be clothed.
They are freezing on the doorstep of the house of my mind.

I am a helpless man—my hands tremble.
I feel in the darkness but cannot find the doorknob.
I look out at the window.
Many tales are dying in the street before the house of my mind.

A New Testament, 1927

THE MAN IN THE BROWN COAT

Napoleon went down into a battle riding on a horse.
Alexander went down into a battle riding on a horse.
General Grant got off a horse and walked into a wood.
General Hindenburg stood on a hill. The moon came up out of a
   clump of bushes.

* * *

I am writing a history of the things men do. I have written three such
   histories and I am but a young man. Already I have written three
   hundred, four hundred thousand words.

My wife is somewhere in this house where for hours I have been sitting
   and writing. She is a tall woman with black hair, turning a little
   grey. Listen, she is going softly up a flight of stairs. All day she goes
   softly doing the housework in our house.

I came here to this town from another town in the state of Iowa. My
   father was a house painter. I worked my way through college and
   became an historian. We own this house in which I sit. This is my
   room in which I work. Already I have written three histories of
   peoples. I have told how states were formed and battles fought. You
   may see my books standing straight up on the shelves of libraries.
   They stand up like sentries.

I am tall like my wife and my shoulders are a little stooped. Although I
   write boldly I am a shy man. I like being in this room alone at work
   with the door locked. There are many books here. Nations march
   back and forth in the books. It is quiet here but in the books a great
   thundering goes on.

* * *

Napoleon rides down a hill and into a battle.
General Grant walks in a wood.
Alexander rides down a hill and into a battle.

My wife has a serious, almost stern look. In the afternoon she leaves
our house and goes for a walk. Sometimes she goes to stores,
sometimes to visit a neighbor. There is a yellow house opposite our
house. My wife goes out a side door and passes along our street
between our house and the yellow house.

The window before my desk makes a little framed place like a picture.
The yellow house across the street makes a solid background of
yellow.

The side door of my house bangs. There is a moment of waiting. My
wife's face floats across the yellow background of the picture.

General Pershing rode down a hill and into a battle.
Alexander rode down a hill and into a battle.

Little things are growing big in my mind. The window before my desk
makes a little framed place like a picture. Every day I wait staring.
I wait with an odd sensation of something impending. My hand
trembles. The face that floats through the picture does something
I do not understand. The face floats, then it stops. It goes from the
right hand side to the left hand side then it stops.

The face comes into my mind and goes out. The face floats in my mind.
The pen has fallen from my fingers. The house is silent. The eyes of
the floating face are turned away from me.

My wife is a girl who came here from Ohio. We have a servant but
she sweeps the floors and sometimes makes the bed in which we
sleep together. We sit together in the evening but I do not know
her. I cannot shake myself out of myself. I wear a brown coat and I

cannot come out of my coat. I cannot come out of myself. My wife is very silent and speaks softly but she cannot come out of herself.

My wife has gone out of the house. She does not know that I know every little thought of her life. I know about her when she was a child and walked in the streets of an Ohio town. I have heard the voices of her mind. I have heard the little voices. I heard the voices crying when she was overtaken with passion and crawled into my arms. I heard the voices when her lips said other words to me as we sat together on the first evening after we were married and moved into this house.

It would be strange if I could sit here as I am doing now while my own face floated across the picture made by the yellow house and the window.

It would be strange and beautiful if I could meet my wife, come into her presence.

The woman whose face floated across my picture just now knows nothing of me. I know nothing of her. She has gone off, along a street. The voices of her mind are talking. I am here in this room, as alone as any man God ever made.

It would be strange and beautiful if I could float my face across a picture. If my floating face could come into her presence, if it could come into the presence of any man or any woman that would be a strange and beautiful thing to have happen.

* * *

Napoleon went down into a battle riding on a horse.
General Grant went into a wood.
Alexander went down into a battle riding on a horse.

* * *

Some day I shall make a testament unto myself.

* * *

I'll tell you sometimes the whole life of this world floats in a human
face in my mind. The unconscious face of the world stops and
stands still before me.

Why do I not say a word out of myself to the others? Why in all our
life together, have I never been able to break through the wall to my
wife? Already I have written three hundred, four hundred thousand
words. Are there no words for love? Some day I shall make a
testament unto myself.

A New Testament, 1927

ONE PUZZLED CONCERNING HIMSELF

I had been to the flesh pots all night—standing beside them, walking
    back and forth in the moonlight. I had gorged myself. My body was
    distended.

I walked home to the city at dawn.
The moonlight was gone.
The streets were empty.
The voice of a drunken man shouted from an alleyway.

I was smug brother to fat men.
I was tired but fattened.
I had been at the flesh pots.

All night the moonlight fell down like rain on the roofs but I stayed at
    the pots, gorging myself.

In the midst of the night as I walked, feeling myself full and complete,
    a child cried and its little voice, filled with strangeness in the quiet
    place, ran under the low black trees.

The voice found no empty place in me.
There was no vacant place where it could echo and reecho.
I was full and complete.
I had been gorging myself at the flesh pots.

A New Testament, 1927

A VAGRANT

I am become a brightly colored insect.
I am a boy lying by a river on a summer day.
At my back is an orchard.

I look dreamily out over warm stagnant waters. There is a reed grows
out of the yellow mud. In the orchard at my back a hog grunts. An
insect with brightly colored back and wings comes swinging down
stream. He has lived more freely than the waters of the river. I go
with him as I would go in at the door of God's house if I knew the
street in which God's house stands, as I would go into you if you
would leave the door open for me.

A New Testament, 1927

NEGRO ON THE DOCKS AT MOBILE, ALA.

I have given out of the richness of myself to many mornings.

At night when the waters of the seas murmured I have murmured.

I have surrendered to seas and suns and days and swinging ships.

My blood is thick with surrender, it shall be let out through wounds
and shall color the seas and the earth.

My blood shall color the earth where the seas come for the night kiss
and the seas shall be red.

I have come out and I shall go back.

I grew and I shall decay.

I have given myself to days and nights. I have been warm and cold. I
have been asleep and awake.

What you see with your eyes I do not see.

What you have felt with your fingers creeps unasked through my
sleeping body.

I have gone into your days and your poison has not come into me.

Open my body and drink—my soul is wet.

I have absorbed suns and seas and days and your poison has not come
into me.

A New Testament, 1927

WORD FACTORIES

Long ago an old man sat on a log at the edge of a cornfield and talked
    to me of God.
His words leaked away.
They would not stay in my head.
The rustling of the leaves of a tree near at hand drowned his voice.
It ran the scale like the voice of an Oriental.
The little drums in my ears were tickled by rising and diminishing
    waves of sound.

His words ran into the rows of corn and became rows of sounds, an
    army of sounds.
They hopped and ran like little naked children.
He did not teach me much of God but fragments of God's truth clung
    to me.

It fell on me like drops of warm rain out of a wet sky.
Did I not learn from him that words are living, breathing things. They
    are the children of men that have been put to work in a factory.
    Their little bodies have become bent and stooped and twisted.

The female words have found no lovers.
They are barren.
It was not God's wish that it be so.
I am one who would serve God.

Have not my brothers the male words been castrated and made into
    eunuchs.

I would be nurse to many distorted words.
I would make my book a hospital for crippled words.

From this day I shall wear a white garment and deny myself the
    pleasures of the body. The words of old time men have been
    reborn in the factory towns of my country. They are choked with
    smoke and drowned in waves of new sounds. Will you give a word

nourishing food, carry him for a day in the warm body of yourself, as a maid carries with due modesty a babe in her belly.

It is time for the old men to come back out of their sleeping stupor.
They must sit again at the edge of the cornfields.
The words of our lips are being destroyed.
They are undernourished and work in the factories.

There is a tough gnarled new word that has lived for a long time in a corner of my brain. He has set up an insanity there. Sometimes for days I do not dare go near the corner of myself where the word sits crouched, ready to strike, to spring. I start to walk boldly in at the door of my house and then grow afraid and run away.

I run out of the present and into the past.
I run past clanging factory towns, past long bridges, over lakes and seas, into the deserts, into the forests.

It is by chance that I recover and come back into myself.

A twisted word seeks warmth in a corner of my brain. His body is bent and his lips twitch. Something tells me he is the son of an old sweet word born on a hillside long ago in the night.

They have brought the little twisted word into the West. In the service in which they put him the air was bad. The flying end of a broken wheel hit him and broke his back. His body twitches when he breathes. He lives but the air whines and whistles as it works its way through his lungs. He has escaped from his servitude and has got into my brain.

My twisted word will live long enough to breed and to perpetuate his kind.

Bring me quickly the female words that are barren and waiting.

If you do not hurry, my twisted word will die in the corner of my brain.
I am a breeding place for a twisted word.
I await the time of the breeding.

A New Testament, 192

MAN LYING ON A COUCH

I am a tree that grows beside the wall. I have been thrusting up and
up. My body is covered with scars. My body is old but still I thrust
upwards, creeping towards the top of the wall.

It is my desire to drop blossoms and fruit over the wall.

I would moisten dry lips.

I would drop blossoms on the heads of children over the top of the wall.

I would caress with falling blossoms the bodies of those who live on
the farther side of the wall.

A New Testament, 1927

ONE WHO WOULD NOT GROW OLD

I have wished that the wind would stop blowing, that birds would
stop dead still in their flight without falling into the sea, that waves
would stand ready to break upon shores without breaking, that all
time, all impulse, all movement, mood, hungers, everything would
stop and stand hushed and still for a moment.

It would be wonderful to be sitting on a log in a forest when it
happened.

When all was still and hushed, just as I have described, I would get off
the log and walk a little.

The insects would all lie still on the ground or float fixed and silent in
the air. An old frog that lives under a stone and that had opened his
mouth to snap at a fly would sit gaping.

There would be no movement in Chicago, in New York, down by the
stock exchange, in towns, in factories, on farms.

Away out in Colorado where a man is at this moment riding his
horse furiously striving to catch a steer to be sent to Chicago to be
butchered and eaten—

He would stop and the steer would stop.

You and I would walk a little way in the forest or on a prairie and
stop. We would be the only moving things in the world and one of
us would start a thought rolling and rolling down time, down space,
down mind, down life too.

I am sure I would let you do it if later you would be still and keep all
the voices of your mind hushed while I did it in my turn.

I would wait ten lives while others did it for my turn.

A New Testament, 1927

AT THE WELL

In the evening I went to the well to drink again. How my bones ached! All the little nerves and muscles of my body cried out.

I had been fighting with God in the long level plain. I ran and ran into a hot dry place and then God came. I fought with him because of the self-satisfaction I saw on his face.

* * *

Had God been substance, had he been a true man I might have laid hold of him. I wrestled all day with a shadow and when afternoon came God smiled again.

Then I went to the well. A few men and women lay on the ground. How softly they talked! There was a negro and a prostitute and two old men who had been robbers.

It was very quiet and peaceful by the well. My hot weary feet touched softly the ground. About the well trees grew and the grass was green. Horses grazed under the trees.

Shall I go again into the plains to fight the self-satisfied God? It is morning and I am thinking now. At the well the negro, the worn-out woman and the two old men are waiting. Knowledge shines out of their eyes. They stay at the well.

A New Testament, 1927

ANOTHER POET

My life runs out and out—dancing in the light like the tongue of a
    serpent.

It goes out and comes back.
My life is a bearer of poison.

I have gone into the plains to poison the well at which I must drink—at
    which you must drink.

That we must destroy each other is obvious. That does not concern me.
    The old poets knew that. It was whispered in the shadows of sheep
    sheds ages ago.

I have thrust out of myself for another purpose.

I am striving to generate a poison that shall be sweeter than the
    drippings of honey combs, sweeter than the lash of the wind.

A New Testament, 1927

A MAN AND TWO WOMEN STANDING BY A WALL FACING THE SEA

My eyes are very small. I cannot see. I look out through narrow slits
into a world of light. The world is bathed in light. I cannot see.

My fingers clutch at little warm spots on the broad face of the world.
This house is a post stuck in the ground. This tree is a hair growing
on the face of a giant.

I cannot see or feel what life is like. My eyes are but two narrow slits into
which the light creeps slowly, feeling its way. The light from a lighted
world tries to creep into me but the womb of my own life is closed.

I lean against the wall with closed eyes and wait.

Would that the light of life could come clambering in through the
narrow closed gate of myself.

Would that the gate could be broken and light come to flood the dark
interior of me.

A God threw up to me out of the sea a little god and I picked it up.

It was thus I became a holy man.
My journeys began.
Holding the little god in my hands I ran.

I ran through houses, through cities, through towns, through halls,
through temples. I opened doors and went in. I opened doors and
came out. I was a thread held in the hand of a weaver. They wove
me. They wove me. They wove me.

I became a holy man.
Their hands beat me. Their hands flayed me.

I knelt in streets, I knelt in silent hills, I knelt by factory doors, on coal
heaps, at the mouths of mines, on slag heaps.
I crept in at the door of a furnace.

It was then I smelled, tasted and ate.
I have put my teeth in.
Their hands beat me, they flayed me.
Those who knew love and those who were afraid of love flayed me.

The hands came toward me out of the darkness, out of the sunlight.
They beat upon me as I knelt in a church. They crept through walls
into the room where I had gone to sleep. The hands of children beat
me. The doubled fists of men and women beat down upon me.

I became a holy man.
The blood came out of my body. The blood came out of my body as a
stream flows in the sunlight.

The hands flayed me like windmills.
The never ceasing hands beat upon me.
My holiness became an insanity.
It became a joy.
It became a relief.

I clung to the little god flung up to me out of the sea.
I became a holy man.

SECOND WOMAN

I have crept out of the egg into a wide colorful world.
My hands reach feebly up.
All about me is the color, the smell of life.

There is the color of cut hillsides, of ships sailing, of seas, of riotous death.
I am born—why do I not die and become colorful?
I am born—why am I not born?

Why am I grey?
Why do I build me grey houses and cities?
Why do I wear grey colorless clothes?
Why do I walk always in grey streets?
I am born—why am I not born?
I am feeble—why do I not become strong?
I am young—why do I not become old?
I am very old—why do I not become young?

Why do I not die and fade into colorful splendor.

I have come out of the egg.

I am born.
Why am I not born?

A New Testament, 1927

MACHINE SONG

*Song written at Columbus, Georgia, in a moment of ecstasy born
of a visit to a cotton mill. . . .*

It has been going on now for thirty, forty, fifty, sixty years. I mean the
machine song. It began away back of that. I am speaking now of the
great chorus, the grand song.

I am speaking of machinery in America, the song of it, the clatter of it,
the whurrrr, the screech, the hummmm, the murmur, the shout of it.

It was there before the World War, before the Civil War.

The machines talk like blackbirds in a meadow at the edge of a
cornfield, the machines shout, they dance on their iron legs.

The machines have a thousand, a million little steel fingers. They grasp
things. Their fingers grasp steel. They grasp the most delicate cotton
and silk fibres. There are great hands of steel, giant hands.

They are picking up and are handling iron pillars, great steel beams.
The hands are themselves machines. They grasp huge beams of steel,
swing them high up.

Steel hands are tearing up the earth. The fingers reach down through
stone, through clay and muck.

They swing great handfuls of earth and stone aloft. They carry steel
beams weighing tons, running with them madly across a room.

They make bridges. They make great dams. They feed upon the power
in rivers. They eat white coal.

Wheels are groaning, wheels are screeching.

It is good to get these sounds into the ears. It is good to see these sights
with the eyes. See the smoke rolling up, the black smoke. See the fire

belching from the great retorts. The machines are cruel as men are cruel. The little flesh and blood fingers of men's hands drive, direct, control the machines.

The machines wear out as men do. Machines are scrapped, thrown on the scrap heap.

At the edges of American cities you will see fields and gullies filled with iron and steel scraps.

There, in that gully, beneath bushes, overgrown by weeds, is an automobile that, but a year or two ago, slid smoothly over roads at forty, fifty, sixty, eighty miles an hour.

How smoothly it ran, how surely. It carried me from Chicago to Miami.

I was in Chicago and it was bleak and cold there. I wanted the sun. Cold winds blew in from the lake. My bones ached. I wanted the sun. I am no longer young. I wanted the sun.

I got into the machine. It was gaily painted. I tell you there will no man live in my day who does not accept the machine.

I myself rejected it. I scorned it. I swore at it. It is destroying my life and the lives of all of the men of my time, I said.

I was a fool. How did I know it would serve me like this?

I went to lie by the river banks. I walked in fields where there were no machines.

Is the machine more cruel than the rain?

Is the machine more cruel than distance?

Is the machine more cruel than snow?

Is the machine more cruel than the sun?

Now the machine in which I rode so gaily from Chicago to Miami, the long, graceful machine, painted a bright scarlet, now it is on a scrap heap. It is in a gully under weeds. In a few years I shall be underground. I shall be on a scrap heap.

What is worth saving of the machine, in which I rode from Chicago to Miami, passing rivers, passing towns, passing cities, passing fields and forests—what is worth saving of the machine will go into the great retorts. It will be melted into new machines. It will sing and fly and work again. What is worth while in me will go into a stalk of corn, into a tree.

I went in the machine from Chicago to Miami. Bitter winds and snow blew about me. My hands that guided the machine were cold.

It ran gaily. There was a soft murmuring sound. Something within the machine sang and something within me sang. Something within me beat with the steady rhythmic beating of the machine.

The machine gave its life to me, into my keeping. My hands guided it. With one turn of my wrists I could have destroyed the machine and myself.

There were crowds of people in the streets of some of the towns and cities through which I passed. I could have destroyed fifty people and myself in destroying the machine.

I passed through Illinois, through Kentucky, Tennessee, North Carolina and went on into Florida. I saw rains, I saw mountains, I saw rivers.

I had a thousand sensations. At night I slept in hotels. I sat in hotel lobbies and talked to men.

Today I made two hundred and fifty-eight miles.

Today I made three hundred and ten miles.

Today I made four hundred miles.

We were stupid, sitting thus, telling each other these bare facts. We told each other nothing of what we meant. We could not tell each other.

There were fat men and lean men, old men and young men. In each man a thousand sensations not told. We were trying to express something we could not express.

I am sick of my old self that protested against the machine. I am sick of that self in me, that self in me, that self in me, that would not live in my own age.

That self in me.

That self in me.

That self in me.

In my own age.

In my own age.

In my own age.

Individuality gone.

Let it go.

Who am I that I should survive?

Let it go.

Let it go.

Steady with the hand. Give thyself, man.

I sing now of the glories of a ride in a machine, from Chicago to Miami.

Miles have become minutes. If I had music in me I would orchestrate
  this. There would no longer be one field, one clump of trees making
  a wood, one town, one river, one bridge over a river.

An automobile, going at forty, at fifty, at sixty miles an hour, passing
  over a bridge, strikes a certain key. There is a little note struck.

Whurrrrr.

It vibrates through the nerves of the body. The ears receive the sound.
  The nerves of the body absorb the sound.

The nerves of the body receive flying things through the ears and the
  eyes. They absorb fields, rivers, bridges.

Towns, cities, clumps of trees that come down to the road.

A clump of trees comes down to the road just so in Illinois.

A clump of trees comes down to the road just so in Tennessee.

Again in Kentucky, Virginia, North Carolina.

There is a man walking in the road in Kentucky.
There is a man walking in the road in Georgia.
The car passed over a viaduct. It makes a sound.
Whurrrrr.

There are faces seen, a thousand faces. A thousand, a hundred
  thousand pairs of hands are grasping the steering wheels of
  automobiles.

I have lost myself in a hundred thousand men, in a hundred thousand women. It is good to be so lost.

Cattle, standing in fields, beside barns, in Illinois, Kentucky, Georgia, Kansas.

Bridges, rivers beneath bridges, dead trees standing solitary in fields, clumps of trees coming down to the road.

New movement.

New music, not heard, felt in the nerves. Come on here, orchestrate this.

Touch this key—a field.

That key—a sloping field.

A creek covered with ice.

A snow-covered field.

Curves in the road.

More curves.

It rains now. The rain beats against the nose of the car.

Who will sing the song of the machine, of the automobile, of the airplane?

Who will sing the song of the factories?

We are in the new age. Welcome, men, women and children into the new age.

Will you accept it?

Will you go into the factories to work?

Will you quit having contempt for those who work in the factories?

You singers, will you go in?

You painters, will you go in?

Will you take the new life? Will you take the factories, the inside and the outside of the factories, as once you took rivers, fields, grassy slopes of fields?

Will you take the blue lights inside of factories at night as once you took sunlight and moonlight?

Will you take a new age? Will you give yourself to a new age?

Will you love factory girls as you love automobiles?

Will you give up individuality?

Will you live, or die?

Will you accept the new age?

Will you give yourself to the new age?

Perhaps Women, 1931

MORNING IN CHICAGO

Now he goes in where I came out;
And all night long in smoke and noise,
On the endless roofs of my rain-washed town,
A broken silence waits on song.

Five Poems, 1939

ASSURANCE

I have heard gods whispering in the corn and wind;
In my crude times when thoughts leaped forth,
Conquering, destroying, serving steel and iron,
I have run back to gods, to prayers and dreams.
I have dreamed much and have remembered dreams.

Now in this room, a face stands forth,
A narrow face, with many shadows 'twixt brow and chin.
The face half turns,
It tells its tale to me,
Now down the drumming way of time it goes and leaves me shaken here.

Now woman and tall man,
My little brother who has passed away,
Bestow a kiss on me.
Turn quick your face, let what is old grow new.
Strike in the darkness at the horrid lie.
Laugh now and pass along.

I remember you forever for a moment's love.
I pass to you the message in the long relay.
Are you brave—do you dare—will you try?
See, I take the death that came into the room with you.

A face remembered, a desire forgot,
A word caught drifting in the long detour,
A caress to you, a swift hail to you.
Forget—remember—dare to cling to me.
Now wait you in the darkness
Till the moment comes.

Mid-American Chants, 1918

BIBLIOGRAPHY

WORKS BY SHERWOOD ANDERSON

Anderson, Sherwood. "An Apology for Crudity." *Dial* 63 (Nov. 8, 1917): 437–38.

——. *Five Poems.* San Mateo, Calif.: Quercus Press, 1939.

——. "Five Poems." *American Mercury* 11 (May 1927): 26–27.

——. "From Chicago." *Seven Arts* 1 (May 1917): 41–59.

——. *Horses and Men.* New York: B. W. Huebsch, 1923.

——. *Letters of Sherwood Anderson.* Edited by Howard Mumford Jones and Walter B. Rideout. Boston: Little, Brown, 1953.

——. "The Man in the Brown Coat." *The Little Review* 7 (Jan.–Mar. 1921): 18–21.

——. *Mid-American Chants.* New York: John Lane, 1918.

——. "Mid American Songs." *Poetry* 10 (Sept. 1917): 281–91.

——. *A New Testament.* New York: Boni & Liveright, 1927.

——. "A New Testament." *Double Dealer* 3 (Feb. 1922): 64–67.

——. "A New Testament." Sherwood Anderson Collection. The Newberry Library, Chicago.

——. "A New Testament." *Vanity Fair* 28 (Apr. 1927): 75.

——. "A New Testament: III." *The Little Review* 6 (Dec. 1919): 17–19.

——. "A New Testament: IV–V." *The Little Review* 6 (Jan. 1920): 15–17.

——. "A New Testament: VI–IX." *The Little Review* 6 (Mar. 1920): 12–16.

——. "A New Testament: X." *The Little Review* 6 (Apr. 1920): 58–60.

——. "A New Testament: XI–XII." *The Little Review* 6 (July–Aug. 1920): 58–61.

——. "A New Testament: The Builder." *Double Dealer* 3 (June 1922): 311.

——. "A New Testament: A Man Speaks Out of the New Confusion." *Playboy* 2 (First Quarter 1923): 9–11.

——. "A New Testament: No. 13." *Double Dealer* 6 (Aug.–Sept. 1924): 181–82.

——. "A New Testament: Testament One." *The Little Review* 6 (Oct. 1919): 3–6.

——. "A New Testament: Testament Two." *The Little Review* 6 (Nov. 1919): 19–21.

——. *Perhaps Women.* New York: Horace Liveright, 1931.

——. *Sherwood Anderson's Memoirs: A Critical Edition.* Edited by Ray Lewis White. Chapel Hill: University of North Carolina Press, 1969.

——. *Sherwood Anderson's Notebook.* New York: Boni & Liveright, 1926.

——. *A Story Teller's Story.* Edited by Ray Lewis White. Cleveland: Press of Case Western Reserve University, 1968.

——. "Testament (Containing Songs of One Who Would Be a Priest)." *Double Dealer* 7 (Nov.–Dec. 1924): 59–60.

——. "Testament of Two Glad Men." *Double Dealer* 3 (Apr. 1922): 203–5.

——. "Testament: One Puzzled Concerning Himself." *Double Dealer* 7 (Jan.–Feb. 1925): 100.

——. "Testament: Song Number One." *Double Dealer* 7 (Oct. 1924): 15–16.

——. *Triumph of the Egg.* New York: B. W. Huebsch, 1921.

——. *Winesburg, Ohio.* New York: B. W. Huebsch, 1919.

——. *The Writer's Book.* Edited by Martha Mulroy Curry. Metuchen, N.J.: Scarecrow Press, 1975.

OTHER PUBLISHED SOURCES

Anderson, David. *Sherwood Anderson: An Introduction and Interpretation.* New York: Holt, Rinehart and Winston, 1967.

Anderson, Margaret. *My Thirty Years' War.* London: Alfred A. Knopf, 1930.

Bradbury, Malcolm, and James McFarlane, eds. *Modernism: A Guide to European Literature, 1890–1930.* New York: Penguin, 1991.

Campbell, Hilbert H., ed. "Sherwood Anderson: Honeymoon Journal and Other Early Writings, 1904." *The Sherwood Anderson Review* 23 (1998): 49.

Campbell, Hilbert H., and Charles E. Modlin. *Sherwood Anderson: Centennial Studies.* Troy, N.Y.: Whitson Publishing, 1976.

Chase, Cleveland B. *Sherwood Anderson.* New York: Robert M. McBride, 1927.

Duffey, Bernard. *The Chicago Renaissance in American Letters: A Critical History.* East Lansing: Michigan State College Press, 1954.

Fagin, N. Bryllion. *The Phenomenon of Sherwood Anderson.* Baltimore: Rossi-Bryn, 1927.

Fanning, Michael. *France and Sherwood Anderson: Paris Notebook, 1921.* Baton Rouge: Louisiana State University Press, 1976.

Gozzi, Raymond D. "A Bibliography of Sherwood Anderson's Contributions to Periodicals, 1914–1946." *The Newberry Library Bulletin,* 2nd ser., no. 2 (Dec. 1948).

Haught, Viva Elizabeth. "The Influence of Walt Whitman on Sherwood Anderson and Carl Sandburg." Master's thesis, Duke University, 1936.

Kramer, Dale. *Chicago Renaissance: The Literary Life in the Midwest, 1900–1930.* New York: Appleton-Century, 1966.

Lenox, Winfield Scott. "The Significance of Sherwood Anderson's Poetry." Master's thesis, Loyola University, 1961.

Ludwig, Richard M., ed. *Aspects of American Poetry.* Columbus: Ohio State University Press, 1962.

Rogers, Douglas G. *Sherwood Anderson: A Selective, Annotated Bibliography.* Metuchen, N.J.: Scarecrow Press, 1976.

Salzman, Jack, David D. Anderson, and Kichinosuke Ohasi. *Sherwood Anderson: A Writer and His Craft.* Mamaroneck, N.Y.: P. P. Appel, 1979.

Sheehy, Eugene P., and Kenneth A. Lohf, eds. *Sherwood Anderson: A Bibliography.* Los Gatos, Calif.: Talisman Press, 1960.

Stein, Gertrude. *Geography and Plays.* Boston: Four Seas, 1922.

Symons, Julian. *Makers of the New: The Revolution in Literature, 1912–1939.* London: Andre Deutsch, 1987.

Taylor, Welford Dunaway, and Charles E. Modlin, eds. *Southern Odyssey: Selected Writings by Sherwood Anderson.* Athens: University of Georgia Press, 1997.

Townsend, Kim. *Sherwood Anderson.* Boston: Houghton Mifflin, 1987.

Weber, Brom. *Sherwood Anderson.* Minneapolis: University of Minnesota Press, 1964.

White, Ray Lewis. *Sherwood Anderson: A Reference Guide.* Boston: G. K. Hall, 1977.

——. *Sherwood Anderson/Gertrude Stein: Correspondence and Personal Essays.* Chapel Hill: University of North Carolina Press, 1972.

——, ed. *Sherwood Anderson: Early Writings.* Kent, Ohio: Kent State University Press, 1989.

Whitman, Walt. *Leaves of Grass.* Edited by Charles Cullen. New York: Thomas Y. Crowell, 1933.